Robert,
Thanks for your support!
[illegible]

A Prescription for Addiction

One Man's Struggle
with Pain Medication

By Ken Start

A Prescription for Addiction

I have tried to recreate events, locales and conversations from my memories of them. I may have changed some identifying characteristics and details such as physical properties, occupations and places of residence. Some names and identifying details have been changed to protect the privacy of individuals.

Cover design by Jacob Kubon.

ISBN 978-1-939294-28-9

www.splatteredinkpress.com

Dedication

To my father, Clarence Start, and living for today.

For I am convinced that neither death nor life, neither angels
nor demons, neither the present nor the future, nor any
powers, neither height nor depth, nor anything else
in all creation, will be able to separate us
from the love of God that is in
Christ Jesus our Lord.

Romans 8:38-39

Acknowledgments

This book was a challenge and I would like to express my gratitude to many people, but I need to start by thanking my wife, Sheryl. This has been a challenging journey and I struggle to even put into words how to thank you for standing by and believing in me when I did not believe in myself. My living successfully in recovery today, and for the past seven years, is because of your enduring and unconditional love.

I would also like to thank my family—Aaron, Kristyn, Eric, Tillie, Sheri, Jayden, Jackson, Kellen and Decker. It has been a long and difficult journey and I have disappointed you in the past and at times I still frustrate you, but to each I say: I love you more than you will ever know, and never forget how proud I am of each of you. My wife, parents, children, grandchildren and family are my life, and my love is unconditional.

Mom, you have encouraged me, loved me and been there in the rough times and good times. We have cried, laughed and prayed together, and I want you to know how much I love you.

To my in-laws, Jerry (deceased) and Sandee Oosterhart, and Claude and Sandy Christiansen, thank you for your love, continual support, encouragement and constant prayers. I could have not asked for better Christian examples of love, faith and forgiveness.

Thanks to W. Michael Hooten, MD, of the Mayo Clinic in Rochester MN. There are no words to express my gratitude for everything you have done to assist me in becoming successful. As my thanks, I will live my life in a manner that proves your time, trust, patience and investment in my life have been worthwhile. This book was your idea and without you it would never have happened. Thank you for your encouragement, time and friendship.

Thank you to Dr. Thomas Kaye, MD, my family health care provider, for encouraging me, challenging me, calling me out, watching over me medically and going out of your way to help me. You are not only a great doctor, but a friend and I am blessed to have you in my life. Thank you for introducing me to recovery and fanning that flame.

Thanks to Dan Wright, BA, D.A.M.O., for your friendship, genuine care, patience and example. As I look back, the time you invested in me has become a large part of my foundation and recovery. Thank you for being there then when I needed you, and still today I know you are only a call away.

Thanks to Dan Qualls, MA, LPC, who invested so much time and energy into aiding me into becoming a successful individual in education, professional career, recovery, marriage, relationships, and slowly helping me get to know myself after many years of living in addiction.

Thanks to Patti Welborn, RN, BA, CCM, for all your support, encouragement and friendship. Having you as a case manager has allowed me to become the healthy and successful individual I am today. Your professionalism and friendship continues to mean a great deal to me.

Thanks to the Mayo Clinic, Onsite Workshops, and Mary Free Bed for the excellent care and continual support you provide to me.

Thank you to Char, Todd, Patti M. and all of my co-workers at Michigan Rehabilitation Services. You have all played a big role in my recovery and success. Char and Todd, you will never know how much you mean to me and how much I appreciate everything you have done in order for me to be where I am today. To this day, I still hear your voices coaching and encouraging.

To my employer, the Social Security Administration in Muskegon MI, what can I say? I have had nothing but support from each of you—John, David, Kelton, Vicki, Debbie and so many others. I am so thankful for my job and grateful for your patience, support and friendships.

Thank you to my friends in recovery and those who are like me, an addict living in reality. A special thanks to Cathy, Terry, Norm, Sean, Deb, Melody, Jennifer, Gayle, Greg and so many others, because I know you, I am a better person.

Thank you to both Ron and Eddie, two special friends that I consider my brothers.

I would like to thank Tricia L. McDonald of Splattered Ink Publishing for enabling me to publish my book. It was a great experience and I am forever grateful for our friendship. You inspired and challenged me to become not only a writer, but an open, honest, and unconditional friend. Thank you so much for your professional and personal investment.

Finally, I apologize to those who have been with me over the course of the years when I was an active addict, for hurting or taking advantage of you in any way.

Foreword

The long-term use of prescription opioids for treatment of chronic non-cancer pain has risen dramatically over the past two decades. This is the same time period during which many of the events described in *A Prescription for Addiction* occurred.

The increased use of prescription opioids has drawn attention to the growing problem of prescription opioid abuse and addiction which have emerged as major threats to U.S. public health. However, the scope of the problem has been evident for over a decade and one of the major focuses of this book is to shed light on how devastating this problem can be to individuals who suffer with chronic pain. For instance, in 2003, approximately 4% of all Medicaid prescriptions were for opioids. Similarly, population-based survey studies utilizing data for the time period extending from 1998 to 2006, showed that up to 5% of adults in the U.S. reported using prescription opioids, and approximately 2% of U.S. adults, or 4.3 million individuals, were regular prescription opioid users.

During this same time period, sales of hydrocodone increased 244% while sales of methadone and oxycodone rose 1177% and 732%, respectively. Commensurate with increased sales of prescription opioids, the milligram per person (mg/person) use increased 347% from 74 mg/person in 1997 to 329 mg/person in 2006. Increased sales and use of greater quantities of prescription opioids was also associated with an increased number of overdose fatalities [9-11], which increased 91% between 1999 and 2002. In 2007, the number of persons receiving emergency medical care for the misuse or abuse of pharmaceuticals, including prescription opioids, eclipsed the number of persons receiving emergency medical care for illicit drug use.

In the current era, data from the most recent National Survey on Drug Use and Health (NSDUH) suggests the prevalence of prescription opioid abuse among individuals age 12 to 25 years has declined slightly since 2010. However, the prevalence of abuse by adults age 26 and older has steadily increased. This is particularly concerning because persons in this older age category are at greater risk of accidental overdose death. This is the age group that Author Ken Start represents and the events described in *A Prescription for Addiction* show he is fortunate in that he never experienced a near fatal overdose.

Consistent with the sustained prevalence of prescription opioid misuse in the US, the most recent NSDUH data also showed that the number of persons receiving treatment for prescription opioid abuse or addiction increased nearly 300% from 2002 to 2012. In 2010, the most likely indication for substance abuse treatment was alcohol, followed by marijuana and prescription opioids. By 2012, prescription opioids had surpassed marijuana to become the second most likely indication for such treatment. In many ways, the struggles described in *A Prescription for Addiction* closely reflect the problems that have been evolving on eight national scales.

Significant health care resources continue to be allocated toward development of clinical models aimed at improving and optimizing the delivery of long-term opioids to adults with chronic pain. Juxtaposed between these clinical endeavors have been efforts to improve the identification and treatment of opioid abuse and dependence. Rather than continue this vexing expenditure of valuable health care resources, increased emphasis should be placed towards the implementation of effective non-opioid based treatments within the primary care setting where the majority of adults with chronic pain receive healthcare. This could potentially reduce the quantity of opioids that are prescribed and decrease the availability of these medications through healthcare facilities. One of the key factors central to Author Ken Start's success in battling prescription opioid addiction and chronic pain has been a complete acceptance he will always be struggling and having to manage chronic pain for the rest of his life. However, he has identified important non-pharmacological and non-procedural approaches to modifying the course of his chronic pain and associated addiction. In this way, Ken has truly developed critical behavioral adaptations which have not only improved his quality of life but the quality of life of those around him including his devoted wife, children, and extended family.

W. Michael Hooten, MD
Professor
Division of Pain Medicine
Department of Anesthesiology
Mayo Clinic College of Medicine
Rochester, MN

Table of Contents

Look At Me...

Why am I, a former addict, sitting in the front row of a large auditorium at the University of Michigan? The room is filled with doctors, surgeons, numerous medical professionals, medical professors and medical students. There is another auditorium down the hall that holds more attendees, including a few of my family members who will watch the presentation live via streaming video.

I swallow hard, look to my left and feel relief seeing Dr. Michael Hooten, pain specialist from Mayo Clinic, sitting next to me. We have been invited to speak at this conference to shed light on the possible misuse of narcotics and opiates in the medical field—something I know personally. We have presented this information before at other medical conferences, so I have a general idea of the presentation goals, but I still feel anxious.

Dr. Hooten and I are scheduled to be the third presenters, so I watch and listen to what the first two physician presenters believe about the topic of narcotics and opiates and their use in medical treatments. Regardless of their thoughts and beliefs, I know what my experience has been with addiction involving prescriptions that included narcotics, opiates, and countless other drugs.

After the second presentation there is a short break, but I stay in my seat while most in the auditorium file out to get a drink, take a short walk, stretch or answer a phone call. I focus on this moment, grateful for those who helped me get here. People like Dr. Hooten. I breathe and relax before it is my turn to speak.

Everyone returns to their seats and the host of the conference introduces Dr. Hooten. To begin, he shows a short taped interview with me recorded soon after I was released from my eighth drug and alcohol rehabilitation visit at the Mayo Clinic in Rochester, Minnesota. I am embarrassed as I watch the 'onscreen me' brag about finding satisfaction in using and manipulating doctors to get what I needed. It is hard to watch my face light up when I talk about scoring drugs from medical doctors or facilities, even though I know it is common in our world today.

In today's society we have become so used to people using pills and prescriptions, we all know someone who is taking more than they should. You can see it daily in the news, TV, movies, Internet and anywhere you go. So many senseless deaths and suicides are caused by prescription medications and their misuse.

After the video, Dr. Hooten shares his opinion of the use of narcotics, opiates and other prescriptions with acute and chronic pain issues. After he finishes, he asks me to share my story.

I open my mouth to speak, but nothing comes out. I swallow and clear my throat.

"I am an addict," I say. I tell them how I lied, cheated, misused and manipulated anyone I could, including doctors, friends, family, and countless medical professionals, into giving me prescriptions for narcotics, opiates and whatever I could get my hands on.

I see skeptical looks on some of the faces of the doctors in the audience, and my insecurities kick in. *What am I doing here?* I think. I look over at Dr. Hooten and he nods, encouraging me to continue.

"Although you probably won't believe me," I say, "I could probably manipulate most of you into giving me drugs."

Snickers arise from the audience and a few people shake their heads and mumble to the person beside them.

"Why should I listen to advice from a drug addict?" a well-dressed man in the middle of the audience says.

"Why wouldn't you?" I say.

An Accidental Beginning

It was a cold February day in Western Michigan and I had overslept. As I was rushing around, I heard the TV weatherman warn that the previous night's wet roads had turned into a shiny layer of ice. I never worried about the weather, since I only lived a few miles from work.

My wife of eight years, Sheryl, was waking up our five-year old, Aaron, and preparing his favorite breakfast, Fruit Loops and milk. Our youngest son, two-year old Eric, was still asleep. Sheryl ran a daycare out of our home for three children who were in her care by seven in the morning. I kissed Aaron goodbye as he sat at the breakfast nook, gave my wife a kiss and rushed out the door knowing I had 15 minutes to get to work.

Driving to work I thought our son's kindergarten class would probably be canceled as everything was a sheet of ice. Black ice was spotty on the road and I had to use extreme caution and drive slower than normal, even if being late became an issue. I entered a curve in the road and saw another car coming from the opposite direction entering the same curve.

When their headlights began to go from one side of the road to the other, I realized the driver had lost control of his car and I needed to get out of his path. I drove off the road and was in the front yard of a home when I saw headlights coming at me and then heard the sound of our cars colliding.

After impact, I seemed to be okay. The armrest between me and the front passenger seat was bent and there was glass, ripped upholstery, broken trim, and plastic pieces everywhere in the car, on me in my hair and clothes.

As I made my way from the driver's seat across to the passenger's seat, I was met by the other driver who opened the door. He was okay and after talking for a moment, I walked to a nearby gas station and called the police (this was before cell phones). As I walked back to the scene of the accident, I was shocked by the damage to our vehicles.

Although my car was totaled, the other car was still drivable and he was able to drive it to an adjacent parking lot. After receiving a ticket from the police officer, the driver of the other car asked me again if I was okay. I told him if I felt any aches or pains later I would get checked out at the emergency room. He left and the policeman asked me if I needed a ride home. We waited about five minutes until a tow truck showed up. As I watched my car being towed away, the policeman opened the back door of his cruiser and allowed me to get in, shutting the door behind me.

When I walked into our home, Sheryl met me at the door with a gentle hug, not knowing what my injuries might be. I made my way into the living room where I sat and felt twinges of pain in my left wrist, neck and lower back. I just thought that would be normal after being hit like I had been. After letting my employer know what had happened and deciding to take the day off, I contacted my father-in-law in hopes he could help me find a new vehicle.

An hour later, my father in law and I were looking for a replacement family car. During the afternoon I began to feel nauseated and light headed, but since I was convinced I wasn't hurt at the scene of the accident, I didn't go to the emergency room. My father-in-law took me home and I crawled onto the couch where I remained until the next morning.

The next day was Saturday and I was scheduled to work eight hours overtime at the shop where I operated a machine that manufactured Harley Davidson engine components. After a sleepless night, I was so stiff I skipped the shower, wet down my hair, brushed my teeth, threw on some work clothes and grabbed my protective eye glasses. Sheryl woke the boys and got them dressed in order to drive me to work. I walked in stiff, sore and light headed, but thought the two ibuprofen tablets I took before leaving the house would kick in and relieve some of the pain and discomfort, allowing me to work my scheduled shift.

About an hour into my shift I was vomiting, light-headed and so sore I couldn't take it. My foreman found a replacement for me, and my mom picked me up from work and drove me home. I took a hot shower, changed into clean clothes and relaxed in my recliner after taking two more ibuprofen tablets. After a short time, my father-in-law phoned to see if I was still planning to go look at cars that afternoon. I shared what had happened at work and he thought it would be smart for him to take me to see one of his friends, a chiropractor, just to see what he thought. I had met this doctor in the past and at this point I just wanted someone to help me.

He performed an accelerated physical exam and took several x-rays of my back and neck. As I readjusted my body for each x-ray, I felt more and more pain, as well as light-headed and nauseated. It didn't take long before the x-rays were on his lighted display box on the wall where I was sitting in a chair, wrapped in a blanket. The doctor looked at the pictures and stated nothing looked broken or injured beyond repair.

I was relieved, as a serious injury would not fit into my busy schedule as an active twenty-eight year old father, working full-time and attending college. I had no presumptions that anything serious was wrong, but was glad to hear it from a professional. After lightly adjusting my back, neck, legs and arms, the doctor set up a treatment plan that would require me to visit him three times over the next week for minor adjustments and stretches. Back in the car on my way back home, I was relieved to know I was physically okay and this sick feeling was only temporary and just a part of being knocked around in the accident. Within minutes of entering my house I was in bed and resting after taking two more ibuprofen tablets and hoping they would help with some of the pain and discomfort.

Over the next week, I followed through with the chiropractor's adjustments, stretching and light massage. I was taken off work temporarily and continued to take ibuprofen as prescribed on the bottle. However, things were getting worse. After a week, the chiropractor felt it would be a good idea if I was seen and evaluated by an orthopedic specialist.

Three days later I was in the office of a specialist. After speaking with the receptionist, filling out the required insurance papers and questionnaires, providing chiropractor's x-rays, I sat in the waiting room with my wife. I felt stiff, sick, shaky, anxious and scared. We were feeling a bit of stress about my condition, as over the last week I hadn't seen any progress. Hopefully, this appointment and the specialist would be able to give me an idea of what was going on and set a plan that would allow me to improve quicker and get back to work and my life.

In the examination room, after donning a hospital gown, I was asked to bend, twist, walk on my tippy toes, and other normally easy tasks that were now almost impossible. The doctor asked me a lot of questions and then had me lie on the exam table where he manually bent my legs, arms and neck.

After physically examining me, he took a look at my x-rays which were once again lit up on the wall. After looking at the x-rays for a few minutes, he took a seat on his stool and rolled over to where I was seated on the exam table. Although I was feeling pain, stiff, and sickness, he agreed with the chiropractor and stated he felt there was no major damage. He told me it would take time, patience and relaxation for me to start feeling better. He also wanted me to begin massage therapy, ultra sound therapy and hot packs at his office, which his office staff would schedule and get me started right away. At the end of the conversation he added he would prescribe a pain medication and muscle relaxer that should help with some of the discomfort. Little did I know his last sentence and instruction would forever change my life.

Scheduled to start therapy the next morning, I was given two paper prescriptions. I limped out of the door worried this was a much larger problem than I expected, while my wife encouraged me that everything would be okay in time, just like the specialist said. In the back of my mind I thought something didn't seem right, but I now had two opinions that agreed I would be fine given time and patience.

Three weeks later, I returned to see the specialist for the second time. I had not missed a therapy appointment and certainly not missed a dose of the pain or muscle relaxer medication. In fact, I had grown to like the medication and temporary feeling of separation from my mind and body it provided. In just three weeks I had decided I was going to push for an increase in the dosage of both the pain medication and muscle relaxer, not only for the pain but also for the feeling of mental relief it provided. I had never been through an injury such as this and did not know how the doctor would respond. Little did I know how easy it would be; I asked for an increase and received an increase.

That was the beginning of a love relationship that would last for years. At home, I looked forward to pill time and began taking more than I was prescribed, sacrificing some doses so I could increase others to increase the great feeling they provided. Over time I was hiding the pill bottles so my wife wouldn't know I was taking them incorrectly. I was a willing participant in my blossoming addiction. My behaviors, cravings and love for medications were in motion and things would only get worse.

After six months of ultrasound, massage, hot pack therapy, and seeing the orthopedic specialist on a regular basis, I was still feeling pain. That pain had turned me into a man who did nothing but lie on the couch and sit in the recliner. I was depressed, isolated, inactive and moody. I had manipulated my doctor into prescribing me high doses of narcotics and opiates, and fell into using those medications incorrectly. I was even stealing medications from others. I had borrowed a prescription book and would look up medications, find out what their effects would be and if the effects were what I was looking for.

My life had become very sad in a short period of time. I was off work, my auto insurance was paying my wages, and although the pain medications helped, the stabbing, excruciating pain was always present. I had numbness and pain in my left leg, and headaches that just about drove me insane. Six months since the accident and not only did I have physical pain, but emotional pain as well. This pain stemmed from the physical injury, and the unknown factor of why things were not improving. I was taking strong medications both incorrectly and at high doses, and adding others to my regimen, as well.

What a mess this had become and what a mess I had created in just a short time. One day my wife walked from the mailbox and had read a letter from my auto insurance stating they had set up for an appointment with a doctor of their choosing in Grand Rapids. My first thought was they would say I was faking and I would then have to return to work, and I knew that was impossible. Even though I was messing with my meds, I was not faking the injury.

Two weeks later I walked into the Grand Rapids' office stiff, sore, worried, anxious and a bit high from the several pills I had taken just before leaving the house. The pills I had taken were stockpiled just for that appointment. I had stolen them from a loved one's bottle of sleeping pills. So, for that appointment, I was comforted not only by my wife, but also from the effects of pills I had taken incorrectly.

Once the doctor entered the examination room, we went through the day of the accident, everything that happened and how I felt. Next, we covered everything I had done since, the chiropractor and his treatments, then the orthopedic specialist and his treatments and medications. The doctor asked about the medications I was taking and I told him the prescriptions and amounts. I left out that I was not taking them as prescribed, and that I was taking other medications.

After a long conversation, he asked me to take my shirt off for a physical examination. I removed my shirt as instructed, he asked me to stand in front of a floor length mirror on one wall of the exam room and he stepped behind me.

"I believe we have a problem," he said, after looking at me from behind and over my shoulder. He continued to look at my neck, chest and stomach from behind me in the mirror. Finally he came around and stated he felt there may be a problem due to the fact that the hairline that started on my upper chest and ran down my abdomen was not straight, but curved on my stomach. He then completed his physical examination and looked at my x-rays.

He stated he did not like the x-rays due to the fact there was no view of my lower back and he was going to have a few new x-rays taken. About ten minutes after the new x-rays were taken, the doctor walked back in and sat down in an empty chair. He wasted no time in sharing that I was seriously injured in the accident and he believed I had suffered a broken back. I was in shock.

After telling us about the injury itself, the doctor explained it was missed due to the x-rays not covering my lower back. He told us I would have to be seen by an orthopedic specialist who dealt with this type of injury and have it repaired surgically. Thankfully, the name of the surgeon he gave us was Dr. Yousif Hamati, a well-known doctor in Muskegon.

A few days later I was in Dr. Hamati's office and after a lengthy first appointment, and a follow-up appointment, I was scheduled for surgery.

That first back surgery lasted eight hours and included a bone donor, graphing, fusion, screws, rods and other hardware. I was in the hospital a week, and the pain was horrible, but the pain medications were even better. During my inpatient stay, I was introduced to many new medications and their wonderful effects. I was hooked up to a morphine machine that allowed me to decide when I needed a new dose. I had been dishonest with my surgeon about the medications I was taking, how I was addicted to the meds I had been prescribed, the meds I was stealing from others, and the drugs, such as marijuana, I had fallen in love with on the side.

I was becoming an addict. After coming home, I became more and more dependent on drugs. Now, I was seeing a psychiatrist for depression and anxiety, and I learned how to get more drugs that would assist me in getting the effects I wanted.

Dr. Hamati was a smart man, surgeon and professional who knew I could not manipulate him, so I went to others for the drugs I needed. As time went on, I met new doctors and therapists and it became easier for me to manipulate them into giving me what I wanted. I would do my homework and then ask for medications that would allow me to get the high I wanted.

A year after the first back surgery I was back in the operating room having the hardware removed, due to it becoming painful for me. By now I was self-destructing due to the self-medicating. I was dealing with physical pain from the back and leg from the auto accident and the mental pain of anxiety, depression and a life overtaken by prescription addiction. I was taking my medications, those of the people around me who didn't lock them away, smoking marijuana, and not being able to get enough of what I was taking.

I was becoming more and more depressed, more and more hopeless, and the pain was overpowering, both physically and mentally. I was seeing doctors for physical and mental issues, using those doctors for the drugs I needed, and getting more of what I wanted.

A year and a half after my auto accident, as I experienced pain from the initial injury and received new drugs, I was written not one, but several prescriptions for addiction.

As I Watched Him

By Sheryl Start

As I watched him become an addict, I felt powerless. Nothing I did seemed to help. I would get him into rehab and think that would help, but to no avail. He would be okay for a while and then it would start back up and the cycle would continue. I watched as he slurred his words when he spoke to other people and stumbled when he was walking. He had glassy eyes and slept all the time. I tried to protect him and the kids from what others would say about what was going on, and I turned a blind eye to the addiction, in denial with others, defending him and using his back pain to do so.

As I watched him become an addict, I felt angry. How could he do this to himself, to me, and to our children? How dare he? He had checked out of his responsibilities as a husband and father. I was overwhelmed with taking care of our children, our household and working full time. We were supposed to be doing this together. He had promised he would always be there for me. I began to stuff the anger down into the depths of my soul in order to continue taking care of everything and continue to protect my children from seeing their dad in any incapacitated state. I was angry at him for hurting me, but I didn't have time to show it or deal with it. I just kept stuffing the anger down, continuing to take care of everyone else and neglecting me in an effort to always make sure Ken looked good.

As I watched him become an addict, I felt alone. We would make plans to do things with the kids, maybe a night at a hotel, but would have to cancel because he would take drugs all night and be sick the next day and not be able to go. I would defend his decision to use drugs with the excuse that he was in too much pain to go. I was always trying to make sure the kids knew their dad was okay and not let them see what was really happening. I canceled many plans to the disappointment of our children. I would try to make it up to them by taking them to the mall or doing something on a smaller scale. Even though I was doing something with the kids, he was still missing from another outing and I was alone once again. I was alone with decisions to be made about our children's school issues, financial issues, and many other things that should have been discussed together. I felt alone, lost, scared, worried and weary.

As I watched him become an addict, I felt suspicious. The trust I had in him had disappeared. It would be 11:00 pm and he would tell me he couldn't sleep. He would ask me if we needed anything from the grocery store because he could go and walk around there for something to do until he got tired. I would give him a short list, like milk and bread. He would not return for hours and I would lay awake with worry. Then he would come back and bring nothing on my list. I knew he wasn't going to the grocery store. I didn't trust anything he would tell me he was doing by himself. Did he really make it to his doctor appointments? Did I dare let him drive with the kids in the car? How could I trust he was doing anything he said he was going to do? I prayed he would be safe and God would watch out for him when I couldn't be there.

As I Watched Him

As I watched him become an addict, I felt scared and anxious. I was scared something terrible would happen; a car accident, overdose, or suicide. I was so scared to say anything wrong that would send him into a tailspin. I tried to hide any serious dilemmas from him which ended up causing me tremendous anxiety. I would just tell him everything was good and not to worry, but in the meantime I was full of worry. I thought I was doing the right thing by protecting him from any problems.

As I watched him become an addict, I felt embarrassed. He would be at a sporting event for the kids, a family get-together, or at church and be slurring his speech or have bloodshot eyes. I would defend him by saying his back was hurting him worse that day so he had to take extra pain pills. I always tried to make him look good, sometimes at the expense of myself. It was embarrassing to watch him stumble or hear him make an off-color comment. Always his champion, I was ready with an excuse, ready to defend him so nobody would think anything bad about him. He wanted everyone to like him and I tried to make sure they did, no matter what he said or did. I would cringe inside, so embarrassed, but then would jump right up with my defense.

As I watched him become an addict, I felt so unsure. What should I do? How could I help him? What about me and the kids? How could I protect them from seeing what their dad had become? I didn't know where to turn or who could help me. Should I stay with him or take the kids and leave until he found some help? I knew I loved him and if I left he would have no one by his side to help him, but what was the right answer? My faith would not allow me to leave. This was new territory and it was like climbing Mt. Everest. How was I going to traverse this gigantic mountain?

As I watched him become an addict, I felt heartbroken. He had left me, not physically, but emotionally. How could the drugs be more important than me and our relationship? We used to have fun and enjoyed being together, talking and laughing. We could laugh and share so much. How I missed him. It became so lonely without his light-hearted laughter and the sparkle in his eyes. I watched that sparkle disappear, along with his wonderful personality. We had looked forward to holidays with family and friends, but he didn't want to go to any events. He became more and more isolated from me, family and friends. What happened to my wonderful husband who would do anything with me and for me? I spent time alone in tears, frustrated and helpless, lonely and rejected. Drugs had become his new love, and I was not important to him anymore. How could he have cheated on me with drugs?

Throwing My Family under the Bus

I grew up in a family of two older brothers, myself and a younger sister. One brother was six years older, the other was five years older and my sister was six years younger than me. My family was a close knit clan, raised in the Dutch Reformed faith, where family was considered important and God was the center of everything.

I married at the age of 22; my wife, six months older, was both a classmate and friend before becoming my wife. Only fourteen months after being married, our first son was born. Following that, we welcomed another son 20 months later and a daughter almost four years after. I gained a wonderful father-in-law, mother-in-law, and four brothers-in-law, along with their spouses and children. Although my in-laws divorced, they both remarried and their spouses became an important and vital part of my life and recovery. In 2009, we lost my father-in-law, but stayed close with his wife.

Over the years, I lied, manipulated and disregarded any loyalty to my family just to further my own agenda. I hurt these people by my lying, misleading, stealing, being absent, inconsistent behaviors, lack of trustworthiness, manipulation, financial irresponsibility and other negative behaviors.

In 2005, at the height of my addiction, my wife was scheduled for surgery. I was at a work convention 40 miles away, but promised I would get there in time to wish her luck and sit with her mother in the waiting area. That day, like any other morning, I started out with one of my prescription cocktails. From there, I went on with my day, forgetting my wife had surgery until late afternoon. By the time I arrived at the hospital, I went into the restroom and made another prescription cocktail. It was evening and I found my wife in tears, not only from the pain from the surgery, but also the pain I had caused her with my behaviors that day. I had not only missed her surgery, but now I was walking into her room higher than a kite.

On another occasion, I took a prescription cocktail before going to bed. In the middle of the night, I walked into the kitchen, opened the pantry and stood in front of it. My daughter, who was five years old at the time, heard the commotion and walked into the kitchen.

"Daddy, what are you looking for?" she asked.

"I am looking for the painters," I said. "I think they are late."

She was confused with my answer and got my wife.

"Ken, what are you looking for?" my wife asked.

"I am looking for the painters," I said.

My wife calmed my daughter and put her back in her bed. She then marched back into the kitchen.

"Ken, get back to bed and do it now," my wife said.

Sixteen years later, my daughter still remembers this event.

My addiction and foolish behaviors not only caused my children to endure emotional pain, but on numerous occasions, I jeopardized their lives.

While using, I cared only about myself and never thought about how my actions would affect my children. On one occasion, we took a family vacation to Minneapolis, MN. Our plans were to go to the Mall of America and enjoy both the shopping and the inside amusement park. It wasn't bad enough I drove us there higher than a kite, but I once again turned a great experience into a nightmare.

After we arrived at the hotel and began to unpack the van, my wife questioned how many pills I had taken. As always, I played the untruthful card like an ace in the hole and stated I had only taken the prescribed amount, but I took them on an empty stomach, which caused a stronger effect. I had other excuses I used for when people questioned my medications, such as saying I thought I forgot to take my meds as scheduled and was just catching up, when in reality I had taken the regular morning dose. Another excuse was I had missed my last dose so I doubled this dose. On top of the excuses, I was also taking large amounts of pills and alcohol only I knew about.

Needless to say, my wife knew darn well something was wrong. As she questioned me, I became more and more defensive, which resulted in me losing my temper in the hotel room. I became irate and was yelling at the top of my lungs. I told my family to pack the van back up and we were going back home. I then added that when we got home, I was leaving and getting away from them. I added, as martyrs do, my leaving should make them happy because I was just wrecking their lives.

By the end of this scenario, I was sleeping due to the high level of narcotics I took before the argument and my family was trying to recover from the emotional hurricane they had just witnessed.

My family lived like this for fifteen years, and although we do have some good memories, there are those where I, as an addict, took center stage and made a total fool of myself, all the while hurting those closest to me.

My children became used to coming home and finding me in bed sleeping. Mixing drugs and alcohol, I felt tired and relaxed most of the time, which was my ultimate goal. I would schedule my time so I could use the majority of medications and alcohol in the early morning and afternoon, causing me to sleep most of the day. I would then stay up late at night, which would afford me the time and availability to make "runs" to keep the medications coming.

At one time, my youngest son went to the doctor to have a hangnail surgically cared for and came home with a prescription for Darvocet. Although I wasn't looking for it, I found the bottle in his room and took the pills. When they came up missing, it was obvious the person my son trusted for his well-being and safety was the one who disregarded his physical pain and sadly, broke his trust once again.

My children witnessed many of my irresponsible behaviors that brought them hurt, embarrassment, anger, disappointment and loss of trust, but there were also times my addiction put them in harm's way. At times, I was incapacitated due to drugs and alcohol, and I drove with my children in the car.

On one occasion, I ran a red light at one of the main intersections in town. Another time, I was driving down the highway and hit three orange and white construction barrels set up on the road. Since I was taking handfuls of pills and using alcohol, the barrels didn't mean a thing.

Stealing was not beneath me and as evidenced by my son's medication; stealing from my own family was not off limits for me and my addiction.

My father was ill, living with chronic pain and taking multiple narcotics and other medications for his medical conditions. My mother was also taking a low dose of depression and anxiety medication, which made their house an easy target for a thief like me. I used any excuse I could to use the bathroom and then, with the water running to muffle the sound, I would search through the medicine cabinet.

Looking through the medications alone would make my heart race, but stealing from my parents never bothered me. In my sick mind, I thought they would get their prescriptions refilled and never notice the missing pills.

My favorite medication to steal from my parents was Xanax. When I first started taking their medications, I would only take two or three of these pills, but as my addiction grew and I needed more to stay high, I would steal more and more.

One night, after a visit to my parent's home, my mother called.

"Ken, did you take any pills from our medicine cabinet," she asked.

"No," I lied.

"I know you did," she said. They had begun suspecting pills were missing, so they were counting them on a regular basis and had just counted them the day before my visit. I was caught red handed, but I didn't care as there were others not expecting me to look through their cabinets. I would just have to go to other places to look. And I did.

One winter day, my younger son came home from high school with three varsity basketball teammates. My son walked into the house and revealed two clear plastic bags containing marijuana.

"Whose are these?" he asked my wife and me.

My oldest son was married and no longer lived with us, so they didn't belong to him. My daughter was not old enough to drive and had not been in the van, and they didn't belong to my wife.

"They're not mine," I said, with a big smile on my face and lifting my hands in wonder.

"You're lying," my son said as he looked me in the eyes. He threw them on the counter as he and his friends disappeared down the stairs to his room.

As he walked away, I heard him say, "Come on Dad," and by the tone in his voice I knew I had let him down again.

Of course the drugs were mine and I had been made a fool in front of my son's friends, in my own kitchen. What would they tell their parents and how would I look at the basketball games now that others knew? I never gave any thought about how it would affect my son, how he felt at the time, or even how my wife felt.

On another occasion, I stayed with my father-in-law and his wife in Florida, while waiting for an internal morphine pump appointment. I stayed with them on a regular basis while having my pump refilled. Even though my in-laws opened their home and hearts to me, I found a way to manipulate and abuse their trust. I would tell them I needed their van to meet with friends of mine who lived in the area for dinner.

I would take their van, always late in the evening, and meet up with people I had chatted with online to get the drugs I needed to stay high while I was there. I would go to a local bar in either Clearwater or Tampa, get what I needed and head home. After only a few hours I would make a quiet return, let myself into the house and go on as if nothing had happened. I never took into account what could happen if I was stopped by the police with drugs in my possession.

Every visit to Tampa included this violation of my in-laws' trust, in order for me to get what I wanted and needed. It was about how I could keep getting the main ingredients I needed to further my addiction. Even the love my in-laws showed me during a rough time was not enough for me to stop and think about what I was doing.

Against My Will

My long recovery journey brought me to eight inpatient treatment facilities and at least four outpatient clinics.

My first rehab visit was close to thirteen months after my first major back surgery. I had become addicted to painkillers, muscle relaxers and anxiety medications. My family had watched me go from a clear minded individual and active participant in life, to a withdrawn, tired, unpredictable, undependable and moody individual who, at times, could barely hold his head up and speak without slurring his words.

My wife was angry and frustrated with my actions and my behavior related to my addiction. With the responsibilities that come with having three children under the age of six; she needed me to be there both physically and mentally. My parents and siblings had also witnessed me become an individual who was confused, emotional, erratic and unpredictable the majority of the time, unlike the loving and fun individual they had raised and grown up with.

One rainy, cold and wet October evening in West Michigan, I went trick-or-treating with my wife and children. Before we left, I had taken a large amount of painkillers and anxiety medications. My parents had come over to watch our infant daughter and I was holding hands with my six-year-old son, while my wife pulled our red flyer wagon with our three-year-old son as its passenger. After going down three streets of our large sub division, my children were tired from going house to house. My wife thought we should head back so they could change their clothes and warm up. However, I was set on pushing through and stopping only when the allotted time had expired. Being intoxicated with medications, I became adamant that we should pick up the speed a bit. My wife became angrier with each passing minute and the kids, now soaked to the bone, were tired, crying, and wanted to go home. I ignored what was best for them and after two disastrous hours, we began our journey back.

After arriving at home, my wife undressed our children, got them a warm bath and then settled them into bed for the night. My parents gave me a lecture in the entryway of our house about how what I had done was so ridiculous. After listening to them, I took another handful of pills, went to my room and that is where my wife found me passed out a few minutes later.

It's unbelievable a husband and father would put his family through such an experience. It's also unbelievable an individual would become his own pharmacist, taking drugs and making mixtures in unknown amounts without thinking about what a deadly decision it might be. Yet this was my behavior on a regular basis: take drugs, act like a fool, sleep, take drugs, act like a fool, sleep, etc.

My mother became concerned with my erratic behavior that night and before leaving, asked my wife about it. My wife shared she was at her wits end with my behavior and didn't know what to do. She also said I had a scheduled appointment the next day with a psychologist and she was going to ask him about my behavior.

The next day, I found myself sitting in a psychologist's office listening to my wife share my recent behavior, including our trick-or-treat experience. Before leaving the house, I had once again loaded up on medications so I was feeling a bit out of it and only hearing bits and pieces of the conversation. I cared about none of it. After attempting to answer a few questions from the psychologist, I listened to the conversation between him and my wife. I was in my own world, void of reality. It was a world I was beginning to love.

Once we returned home, I went back to sleep. Sleep was a vacation from reality and my constant back pain. After waking, I took a few more pills. Sitting down in my favorite lounge chair in the living room, my mom walked in unannounced and together with my wife, shared we were going to go to an appointment they had made. Being under the influence of pain killers, I never thought to ask what kind of appointment.

I next found myself sitting in a large atrium, like a huge waiting room. I was still feeling the effects of the drugs, so I just sat there as my wife went up and spoke with a woman at a large desk. After a short time, my wife came back to our seats with a nurse. The nurse introduced herself and told me I was going to be staying there for a few days. She stated my family was concerned about my recent mental and physical state and this facility would assist me in feeling better and dealing with the pain I was experiencing, both physical and mental. At that point, my wife and mother stated they were leaving and would be back to visit when the facility allowed.

What just happened? I was in an unknown place and told I would be there for a few days. I was high and feeling the effects of my last dosage of pills, so this experience felt surreal. *Is this happening? Me, an elder at my church, being hospitalized for addiction issues?* Did I want to do this? Did I have a choice? Where was I? What kind of place was this? What did they do here? What was expected of me? These questions were going through my head, along with the biggest question—where would I get my pills? Those were my magic pills that I was falling in love with and couldn't live without.

As the nurse and I stood in the atrium, my wife walked back in with a duffel bag and a pillow and gave them to me. She kissed me with tears on her cheeks and walked out. The nurse asked me to follow her as she began walking in the direction of two large doors which would lead me to the beginning of a long chain of treatment attempts.

In order to enter the actual treatment facility, the nurse had to ring a buzzer and have authorization to enter. After a short conversation through an intercom, the doors clicked open. As we began walking down the hallway toward our destination, I heard the doors click and lock behind us. I had always thought lock-down institutions were for people who were sick and dangerous, and now I was in one of them.

I was instructed to take a seat near the nurses' station, as she retrieved the materials needed to register me as a patient. As I sat there with my duffel bag and pillow resting in the chair next to me, I looked around. Part of this large room was the nurses' station and the other part was partitioned off with a half wall which appeared to have shelves and drawers built into it. There was an entry way into the partitioned part of the room and it looked like an area used for eating and socializing. I could see several individuals sitting on couches and lounge chairs, watching television, reading and relaxing.

The nurse came back and I grabbed my belongings and followed her down the hall, where I was ushered into a small room where she shut the door behind us. She stated a physical examination would be conducted and asked me several questions about my physical and mental conditions.

The nurse then unlocked a cabinet and pulled out a gown, the type you wrap around yourself for a physical examination. She told me she would step out of the room for a few minutes and I was to totally undress, put the gown on and she would be back.

As promised, in only four to five minutes she tapped on the door, walked back in, weighed me and took my vitals. She asked me about my physical history, along with questions about my mental state. I shared information about my auto accident and subsequent back surgery. I told her I was feeling depressed due to the chronic pain. At that point, she asked if I had felt as though I was going to hurt myself. I told her although I had never felt that way in the past, with my current pain issues and depression, it had crossed my mind.

"Have you ever made a plan to hurt yourself," she asked.

"No," I said. However, the thought of suicide would now find its way into my mind more and more and become a demon I would have to deal with in the future.

After she completed this part of the examination, the nurse left to get the attending physician to come in and conduct the physical examination. As she left, I sat on the examination table somewhat relaxed from my last dose of narcotics, my eyes focused on the floor and my feet swinging back and forth. The door opened and an older gentleman, I would say in his 60's, walked in and mumbled something. Wearing a white lab coat, he stood and as I sat on the table, he grabbed a silver utensil off a large metal tray and began testing my reflexes: knees, ankles, elbows and hands. Next, he felt my neck, arms, and looked at my back. Saying nothing, he grabbed a light and asked me to open my mouth and then checked my ears and eyes.

After completing the physical examination, he wrote notes in a chart and was about to open the door to leave, when he looked up at me.

"You can get dressed now," he said. "A staff member will be in to get you in a few minutes."

I was quick to take the exam gown off and put on my own clothes. I was feeling lost and like I was in a mess just getting worse. I was taking too much of the prescribed medications, stealing other people's medications and loving it. I was beginning to know how to manipulate doctors to get what I wanted and feeling good about my successes. Still, I sat there wondering where I was going with it.

A few minutes later, a woman came in holding a folder. She laid the folder down, stated her name, and said she was going to assist me with the appropriate paper work, would show me to my room, and then give me a tour of the facility. Being under the influence of my last dosage, all the paperwork and forms made no sense to me and I just signed them. I noticed one form stated I came to the treatment center on my own will and I was not forced, and the other papers were insurance forms. As she talked all I heard was "blah blah blah."

Now that the paperwork was finished, she stated it was procedure to check my duffel bag and pillow for anything not allowed in the facility for safety and security reasons, such as drugs, alcohol, electronics and anything that could be used to hurt myself or others. She took my razor and electric hair dryer my wife had packed and stated they would be returned to me when I was released. I was so foggy I didn't care what they took; I was just confused and anxious. I wanted something that would feel comfortable, like another dose of narcotics to transport me into a land where everything was comfortable and put me into a deep sleep.

The staff member then asked me to follow her and she would show me to my room. As we walked past the large nurses' station and community room, I saw plenty of others, some looked like team members and others were dressed in sweatpants and sweatshirts. Some were wearing slippers, which led me to assume they were other patients. We walked down a long hallway and after we passed a few rooms where it appeared others were staying, she entered into a dark room that would be mine.

The room had a twin size bed, a nightstand with a Bible placed in the drawer, a television located high on the wall opposite the bed, a portable table that went up and across the bed, a built in closet and four drawers for clothes and personal items. Luckily, the room had its own bathroom and a window that allowed light in.

She told me to leave my items in the room and took me on a tour of the facility. We were located in the men's wing of the facility, which was a dead end, so we started walking in the direction of the nurses' station. As we stood in front of the nurses' station, she told me this was the center of the facility. As she pointed to the long hallway on the other side of the nurses' station, she pointed out the women's wing and said I was not allowed to pass the nurses' station going in that direction. We then walked into the large community room. One end of the room was the patient's lounge where we could watch TV, read or relax. She then walked to the other end and we walked through a door and entered a kitchen area. She shared this was the patients' kitchen and I could use it at appropriate times. I was also told there were crackers, some cookies and coffee and tea I could have at any time. Otherwise, everything in the kitchen belonged to the individual whose name was on it.

We then walked out of the kitchen and I followed her to another large room off the community room with four large tables in the center, creating a large rectangle and chairs placed around the tables. Cabinets and counters were placed around the room and there was a double sink. The team member stated this was the activity room where they made crafts.

As we walked out of the activity room, we once again passed the nurses' station and went down the hallway I had been in when I had my physical examination, opposite the community room. Across the hall were two rooms used for group sessions. They had about ten chairs placed in a circle and a bit further down the hallway on both sides, were small rooms with desks and chairs used for patient meetings with doctors and the medical team. That was the end of the tour.

I was told I could take some time to settle into my room and lie down for a while, if I wanted. She would come get me in a while and explain the facility's purpose, and get me in one of the therapy groups scheduled for the next morning with one of the psychiatrists and medical doctors.

As I walked toward my room, I could feel the eyes of the other patients follow me. I entered my dark room, lit by the light streaming in from the hallway, walked to my bed and sat down. My thoughts immediately went to the question of when they would be handing out the next dosage of drugs. Not only was I feeling lower back pain, but I was coming out of my current buzz.

Control was important to me; I wanted control of my surroundings, emotions, agenda and most important, my medications. At that time, I was feeling agitated due to losing control of almost everything and not knowing what was going on. How had I gotten into this situation and when would I get out?

What Was My Reality?

As I sat on my bed; I rested my head in my hands and felt like I was living someone else's life. I had heard of people who had emotional and drug issues and were hospitalized in a ward much like this, but that was not my reality and not me. I was brought up in a Christian home by strict and loving parents with Christian morals, values and a loving family. I had witnessed firsthand the value of hard work, honesty, faith in God and importance of family. I had never met an individual who had dealt with a drug or alcohol issue, or perhaps I should say I never realized I had.

I always believed people in these types of places and with these types of problems were lazy, homeless, drunks and crack heads, who just didn't have the initiative to change. Now, here I was: emotional, broken, depressed, and lost, with a prescription drug addiction. How did this happen? I couldn't answer that question but knew I was beginning to feel the need to take more meds to feed my growing addiction.

I sat deep in thought and pondered my situation for what seemed like minutes, but was actually an hour. The voice of a new team member who entered my room and introduced herself brought me back to reality. She asked me to follow her.

She led me to a conference room where I sat in an uncomfortable chair next to the desk where she talked to me about what was going on. I attempted to listen to what she was saying and look at the folder she had laid on the desk, a folder with a picture of the facility itself on the front of it. She opened the folder and started to go through the papers in it, one at a time.

All I could focus on was the back pain from the uncomfortable chair which was the hard type of chair you find in any doctor's examination room, and the question of when I would get my next dose of pain medication. Even though she was polite, all I heard was blah, blah, blah, until I heard the word medications. At this time, I woke out of my boredom to hear her explaining when and where they handed out the medications. They were handed out by a registered nurse on the far side of the nurses' station at exact times and she emphasized I was to be there at the times and wait in line with the other patients in order to avoid confusion.

While I was still attentive, she explained there were therapy groups I was to attend three times a day and I was expected to participate. She explained these therapy groups were led by a professional counselor and their purpose was to aid each patient, such as myself, with what they were dealing with. I was surprised to hear not each patient was dealing with the same issue. She explained some patients were there due to addictions such as drugs and alcohol, however, others were there due to mental issues such as depression, anxiety, bipolar disorder, suicidal thoughts and ideation.

I learned I would get my first dose of medication before I went to bed, which would be soon since it was close to 9:30 pm. Feeling somewhat better knowing my next high was only a few minutes away, I decided to be adventurous and walk into the community room to get a sense of the atmosphere of my new surroundings.

As I entered the room, I felt the eyes of the others focus on me. As I looked back, I saw empty stares, depressing frowns and one smile. Seconds later, the focus was no longer on me. Two men were sharing a cup of coffee at one of the large tables, two men and a woman were watching television, one woman was working alone on a puzzle, and one man was looking at a newspaper.

I made my way to the kitchen area and made myself a cup of tea. Walking around in this ward and not knowing a soul, I realized I was here alone and on my own. As I began to sip my tea, I made my way out to the nurses' station where they would, in a few short minutes, give me what I needed to relax and make this experience bearable. Just the thought of the upcoming high gave me a rush of excitement. I found a seat close to the nurses' station and decided to stay put until they dispensed the medications.

Not long after taking a seat, the other prisoners began to gather around the area and created a line. Besides those I saw in the community room, there were several others who came out of hibernation to get their nightly doses of medication. Up to this point, not one of the other patients acted as if they saw or noticed me as a new member of their community. They walked right on by as if I was not even in their presence. I didn't expect a ticker tape parade, but a greeting or even a nod of one's head, would have helped me with the feeling of being alone.

As I made my way to the end of the line, I felt a soft tap on my shoulder. Turning around, I saw the woman who was working on the puzzle and who had been the only one to smile at me earlier in the community room. Her smile would stick with me for years. Linda introduced herself and as we walked toward the line she shared that she had been in the facility for a week and knew what it felt like to be new.

Linda was in her mid-forties and heavy set. Her greasy gray hair fell to her shoulders with bangs held up with bobby pins. She wore a red sweatshirt and her navy blue sweatpants looked as though she had worn them several days. Her teeth were bad and she smelled like a perfume my grandmother had preferred twenty-five years earlier, but Linda was talking to me and I was thankful.

As we stood at the end of the line together, Linda shared that she was divorced and had three children, but her mother currently had custody of her children. As we moved closer to the nurse dispensing the drugs, Linda added this was her third hospitalization in the past two months. Just before she presented the nurse with her hospital identification wrist-band and name, she looked at me and said she had attempted suicide twice by overdosing and was here to get help with her bipolar disorder condition.

I showed the nurse my hospital identification wristband (I didn't remember putting on) and stated my name, along with my birth date. Linda was walking toward the community room as the nurse gave me a small Dixie cup with two pills in it. I recognized the pills as Vicodin, a narcotic pain killer. I asked the nurse if she had given me the correct cup and hoped she had made a mistake. The nurse stated this amount was what the facility's physician prescribed for me to take. I looked with disbelief at the little flowered Dixie cup.

What was happening? How was I going to get the buzz I needed in order to settle down for the night? The dosage I received was not even enough to adequately treat my back pain, let alone provide me with the relief from chasing the high.

"Do you think I could at least get one or two more pain pills, like Demerol or Vicodin, and maybe one or two

Klonopins or Xanax," I asked, "just to help me with the pain and allow me to sleep in these new surroundings?"

"I have to follow the doctor's orders," she said. "You'll be able to talk to a doctor in the morning during your evaluation. I can't do anything to change the prescription right now."

I took the two lousy pills in the Dixie cup and chased the pills down with water.

I was frustrated, lost and betrayed. No one had said anything about changing my meds, and I never gave any thought to the fact I was not taking anything as prescribed. Over the past year since my first surgery, I had become my own pharmacist and never thought about the possible consequences. Now, here I was taking what the doctor prescribed and not feeling a thing. I had built up my tolerance level and now needed more meds to feed the addiction.

I thought of how my wife and mother hadn't shared with me that they were taking me to a treatment center. Why would they just put me in a car, drop me off and leave? At that moment all I could think of was ME. What was I going to do? How was I going to get what I wanted? When would I get out of here and return to MY own way of doing things?

The more I thought of the mess I was in, the angrier I became. I knew I had to do something, but wasn't sure what it would be. I turned to talk to the nurse again but she, the tray with pills, and the water cups were gone. I walked to my room angry, sore, confused, frustrated and not sure how to handle any of these feelings and emotions without the medications I wanted and deserved.

As the lights in the facility turned off I began to panic. How would I relax or sleep without my medications? Sitting on my bed, I focused on the drugs I was not being given. I didn't think about my wife, my three small children, my parents, money, bills or my home. All I thought about were the drugs I had fallen in love with.

I wanted to call to my wife, not to ask how she was, but to tell her to come and get me out of here. Unfortunately, the only phone available to me was a wall mounted phone next to the nurses' station, which was only turned on at certain times of the day.

Making things worse, the two Vicodin I had taken were not providing me with even a slight buzz. Feeling agitated, I decided to walk to the kitchen area to see if I could at least get a cup of tea. Caffeine would be a better drug than the two lousy Vicodin; even four bags of Splenda© would do more for me at this moment.

As I made my way out of the kitchen and into the community room, I saw another inmate sitting in the dim light, watching a late night talk show. After sitting on the vacant couch, I looked over and nodded at him as he sat in one of the lounge chairs across from me, holding the remote control. Instead of nodding back, he got out of his chair, and approached me with his left hand extended.

"I'm Jerry," he said. "Glad to meet you."

Jerry was in his mid to late thirties, almost six feet tall and slender with short brown hair, and a full beard, which was trimmed and clean. I was taken back a bit by Jerry's outgoing personality, but appreciated his warm greeting. He sat back in his chair, pointed the remote at the television and turned it down a few levels.

"Where are you from?" he asked.

"I'm Ken," I said, "and I'm from right here in Muskegon."

We both watched the television for a few moments and then Jerry asked me another question and I shared with him my life in general, including my injury, surgery, pain, family, work and current physical and addiction condition.

When I finished, Jerry shared he had never been injured in an accident, he didn't have an addiction issue, he wasn't suicidal and he did not have a mental illness. He stated he had to be here in this institution for one reason and one reason only. I asked him about the reason and he stated it was a private issue and he could not tell me.

I figured he had a personality problem, extreme mental issue or was downright lying to me because there had to be a reason an individual would end up in this place. It wasn't the kind of place you visited for the food, nor was it a five star hotel, where you would spend your vacation time. I didn't know what was up with Jerry, but there was a reason he was here with me.

After three hours of talking with Jerry, I decided it was time to try to get some sleep. I told Jerry good night and began my way back to my room in the dim lit and quiet halls. As I was walking, I felt extreme lower back pain and I realized I was not feeling the buzz I was used to feeling. Talking with Jerry had helped distract me from thinking solely about my pain and addiction issues.

Now back in my room and lying on the top of my bed with my street clothes on, I began to focus on the back pain and lack of a good buzz. The more I thought of how I landed here and lost control of everything, the madder I got. My mind was back on me and it began spinning like a hamster running on his little wheel, thinking about how I ended up in this place. The more I thought about it, the more I felt as though I was going to explode inside. I was hurting physically and mentally and needed my drugs back. I decided I would once again attempt to ask for some type of pain killers to assist me in handling the pain and give me a buzz.

Only a minute or two later, I was at the nurses' station looking into the eyes of an stern looking nurse who did not look happy to be bothered at this time of night.

"Can I help you with anything?" she asked.

"I'm having a lot of lower back pain and was wondering if there is something I can get for it and to help me sleep?"

She walked over to a desk, looked at a chart, and then walked back to me.

"You have nothing more prescribed until morning."

"Is there anything I can take? Even a few ibuprofen?"

"Nothing has been prescribed," she repeated. "You'll have to wait until morning."

I turned around to walk to my room feeling so frustrated I wasn't sure what to do with myself. Should I go to my room and attempt to lie down again? Why? I knew I couldn't sleep with the amount of pain I was experiencing. As I stood there I saw the shadows of the television in the community room and decided I might as well go watch it. Walking around the corner of the community room, I saw Jerry still sitting in the same lounge chair, now half asleep. As I walked in, he sat up a bit and fully opened his eyes.

"So you can't sleep, huh?"

"This place sucks!" I said.

Jerry giggled and said something under his breath. After a moment, he said, "It only gets better friend."

I stared at the television screen.

"You have to be able to play with the big boys here, friend," he said.

What the heck did "play with the big boys" mean? After a few minutes of just watching a silly infomercial, I asked Jerry what he meant by his last statement.

"You have to know what you want and know how to get it," Jerry said as he looked at me square in the eye.

He was beginning to pique my interest. What was his one and only reason for being here and what did he mean by you have to know what you want and know how to get it?

"What do you mean by that?" I asked.

Jerry sat up in his chair, looked straight into my eyes and asked if I was here to rid myself of prescription medications, or if I really believed I needed them to live the quality of life I wanted with my back injury.

What does it matter what I want? I thought. I wasn't here to make me happy, I was here to please my family or at least, get them off my back. Not to mention taking prescription meds not according to doctor's orders was not right or ethical, especially for this young, Christian man. But once again, this man piqued my interest and I was beginning to like the way he challenged me. Jerry was the first individual I had met, other than some doctors, who made getting the pills sound like a viable option.

Even though I had fallen into addictive behaviors, due to the back injury and the love of the high, I didn't think I was at the level Jerry was speaking of. I had squeezed some pills out of a doctor, but nothing that would get me where I thought I was going. However, listening to Jerry, I was getting a feeling of total joy and excitement. It was much like hanging on every word of a motivational speaker, believing you could reach the pinnacle they were speaking of and become more than what you were. I wanted to hear more from Jerry.

"You have to know what you want," Jerry said. He then shared his reason for being in this institution. He stated he could not hold a job, but needed a steady income and had thought of a good way to get it without working. I listened as he talked about his high goal of applying for and being awarded Social Security benefits for depression and suicidal thoughts, even though he had never suffered from depression nor had he ever been suicidal.

Jerry sat back in his chair and stated that in order to receive the benefits, he had to have a severe physical or mental condition. He figured depression and suicidal thoughts would be easier to use than a bad back, since they could not prove he didn't have a mental illness and a simple x-ray would show he had a normal and healthy back. I sat there in the dark, with the television light flickering, shocked anyone would fake an illness and be admitted to an institution to get Social Security benefits. I didn't know what to say or how to respond.

After several seconds of silence, Jerry began explaining he needed to have a couple of visits to a place such as this on his medical records, in order to be awarded the steady benefits. In addition, he knew he had to play his cards right with the doctors, psychologists and medical professionals to be successful.

I was in a bit of shock. Did he really admit himself to this institution and fake his conditions just to manipulate the situation for his own good?

It took a few minutes for this information to register with me and I stared at the television screen. I started wondering how this could work for me. How could I use this information to get more powerful, mind altering, pain relieving, sleep aiding and buzz causing meds from the medical professionals I was going to see in this facility?

Jerry was now asleep sitting in the chair adjacent to me so I decided I would go to my room again. As I was leaving, I noticed it was almost five o'clock in the morning. In my room, I lay on my bed and stared at the ceiling thinking about the conversation I just had with Jerry. I needed to chat with him so I could be prepared for the time I had with the doctors in order to get the most meds from them.

Lessons in Rehab

I woke to a bright light coming from the fluorescent lights in the hallway. I learned that in rehab, you woke early and were expected to be clean, presentable and ready to face another day by 7:00 am. Another thing I learned was the food, which came on trays with your name tag on it, was not good.

I took my tray and sat next to the one person I knew, Jerry, who looked as tired as I felt.

"When do we get our morning meds," I asked, "and when do I see a doctor?"

"Just sit down and relax," he said. "Around here, everything takes time and you might as well get used to it."

I sat next to him and began eating my bowl of Special K cereal. Jerry introduced me to the two other men who were eating their bland looking oatmeal. Both men looked up, nodded their heads in my direction and went right back to eating.

While wiping his hands on a napkin, Jerry asked me about my back injuries and what had happened in the car accident I was involved in. I shared that I had been broad-sided, broke my back and had a surgery about a year earlier. I added I had a bone donor, metal plates and screws and it took a considerable amount of time to heal from the surgery.

"So what meds were you given?" Jerry asked, "And how did you get hooked on them?"

"The first pill I took was a Vicodin and it put me in heaven," I said. Even though the effect was mild, I had fallen in love with the euphoric feeling it provided. I loved the pain relief the little white pill provided, the relaxation it granted and the feeling of just being content with everything.

Just talking about my experiences with drugs over the past year put my mind in touch with a deep craving for another high. I was not as used to going without it, as I was used to taking a small handful of pills every time I began to feel reality set in. I had gone from one white pill, to four or five at a time, plus a muscle relaxer one of my physicians had prescribed. Although I was prescribed one or two of those pills, I took more than was prescribed. Before I knew it, the small handful of pills was becoming larger and larger.

"I started needing more and more to chase the high I first fell in love with," I said to Jerry. "So I bought a prescription manual at the bookstore that explained the different medications and the effects one could expect from taking the listed prescription medication." With my newly found knowledge, I went to the homes of friends and family and searched their medicine cabinets for anything that would assist me in reaching my ultimate goal, which of course, was to get high. I had been rewarded in my adventures, as I found normal size pills, big horse size pills, and capsules. I was like a kid in a candy store. I also knew I didn't want anyone to know what I was doing, so at first I was pretty conservative on how many I took from each bottle. But as time went on, I became more aggressive and took more and more. I didn't feel bad about stealing the pills, as I didn't see it the same as stealing money, jewelry or expensive electronics. My thought was their health insurance would just replace them, if they even noticed they were missing.

I finished my story just as an announcement to line up for morning meds came over the intercom. I could not get to the nurses' station fast enough. However, once again, the little Dixie cup only contained two pills. I recalled seeing these pills in the past and though I was not sure what they were, I did not hesitate to take them. After swallowing them and chasing them down with water, I asked the attending nurse what I had just taken. She checked my chart and then told me I had just taken two Flexeril, muscle relaxers. *Big deal*, I thought. *I just took two muscle relaxers.* I needed much more than that to live a happy life.

As the others in line took their meds and headed to therapy like a herd of cattle, I slipped away from the group and into my room to lie down. I felt frustrated, mad, betrayed, alone and almost sober. With my eyes closed, I raised my hands over my head, and then rested them on my forehead. *Screw group therapy*! Just then I heard someone scuffling down the hallway in my direction and a man in a blue suit walked into my room and asked me my name.

"Ken," I said.

"My name is Dr. Johnson," he said. He was short in stature with dirty blond hair he combed over from one side of his head to the other, even though he had a full head of hair and no bald spot to hide. He wore gold metal rimmed glasses and his navy blue suit looked like it was two sizes too large for him.

"Ken, follow me," he said. So I followed this awkward man past the nurses' station and into a small conference room.

Dr. Johnson sat at a small desk in the room and I sat across from him in an uncomfortable lounge chair. It was quiet and all I could hear was the buzzing of the lights overhead. As Dr. Johnson looked through my chart, I thought about everything Jerry had said the night before. His words, "You have to know what you want when you meet with the doctors," ran through my head. I thought about the things I could use to get what I wanted like pain, surgeries, depression, anxiety, sleep issues, mood swings, relationship issues, and pure and utter sadness. How could I turn these things into drugs? What did I need to say and how did I need to say it to get wonderful little pills and capsules.

I was beginning to feel a little uncomfortable since the doctor had not said a word nor looked up at me since we entered the room. I was used to doctors taking charge of the conversation and appointment right from the start. My back surgery had been performed by a take-charge physician and I always knew what he was thinking, as he was vocal and never failed to look me in the eye while he was talking.

While Dr. Johnson continued to look over the chart, I started running scenarios through my mind that would suggest to him things were a bit worse than they were.

Even though I lived with a large amount of pain, I decided to knock my game up a level or two by stating I could not live with the current level of pain. This was not far from the truth, but I still decided I was going to escalate my pain a level or two, in order to get what I wanted.

I also decided depression was now an issue I needed to elevate in order to get what I wanted. Little did I know, this would come back to bite me later and would almost cost me my life. However, at this moment, I decided to play it up and act as if my depression was severe and I needed help with it, in order to function on a daily basis. This ran through my head during the time it took for the doctor to look at my short file. I was already an addict in the making at that point: dishonest, selfish and manipulative. I knew what I wanted and I was willing to do what it took.

The doctor lifted his head and looked my way, not at me directly, but in my general direction. He cleared his throat and asked me why I was here. *Why am I here?* I thought it was obvious why I was here. My family did not like how I was acting.

"I was involved in an auto accident about a year and a half ago and had a serious lower back injury," I said. "I had spinal fusion with plates and screws a year ago and have lived with severe and agonizing back pain since. In addition, I have been dealing with severe depression on a daily basis that has caused me to think my future is hopeless. "

As the last sentence slipped out of my mouth, I wondered if I had played it up enough. Did I sound believable? I then decided to ask about the medications or lack thereof. I shared with the doctor that I was taking more meds at home then what they had given me here over the past sixteen hours. I added I was concerned about the pain which had kept me from sleeping.

The doctor asked me questions about the accident, surgery, pain, depression, family issues, and my behaviors while taking meds. I answered the question about my behaviors and shared I was not used to taking these medications and had some mild side effects, but there was nothing to worry about. In fact, I added, the level of the prescription was not even close to covering my pain.

I answered his other questions and used the opportunity to focus on how bad my depression had been lately. I laid it on thick about how the depression was due to the pain, not working, feeling like a failure to my wife and three young children, and my unknown and uncertain future. Although I had answered the questions about the accident, surgery and some of the family issues, we spent far more time talking about my pain and depression. I manipulatively answered each of his questions and told the doctor what I wanted him to know.

Finally, he stated he was going to reevaluate the med list my wife had supplied when I was admitted. He would look at changing a few of the meds and maybe adding one or two. He also stated the nurse would give me some of the pain meds I had missed, now that he had seen me. He finished by stating he wanted me to attend the therapy groups, take the scheduled meds, get used to the environment and he would see me again tomorrow.

He got up from his chair, opened the door and walked me across the hall to the nurses' station, where he went behind the desk with my chart and asked for my nurse to join him in the room marked pharmacy. Only a minute or two later, the nurse walked up to me with a Dixie cup and I swallowed the six additional pills. I recognized some of them as Vicodin and I didn't care about the rest. I knew they couldn't hurt, they could only help.

I then followed the nurse to the therapy room and noticed butterflies in my stomach. *Therapy room? What does that mean?* I had never been in a therapy room or therapy group and wasn't sure I wanted to be either. The nurse knocked on the door, opened it and walked in. I followed behind her and when she stopped only a few feet into the room, I did as well. The group leader, Keith, a man in about his thirties, looked up at the two of us.

"Do we have a new member?" Keith asked.

"Why yes we do," the nurse said.

"What's your name?" Keith asked as he shook my hand.

"Ken," I said.

Keith asked me to sit in the only empty chair in the circle of ten. I recognized a few of the faces from out in the community room, but no one I had met or spoken with. Jerry was not in my group but I was wishing he would be there so I would at least know someone.

Keith shared with me that the group would meet every day and chat about what issues we were dealing with and how we were feeling in general. He said he did not want to make me feel uncomfortable, so he would let me introduce myself and meet the others in the afternoon session and share something about myself at that time.

I was feeling sober and didn't like to deal with reality while sober, so I was happy with Keith's suggestion. Hopefully in the afternoon session I would be feeling more intoxicated.

Keith continued on from where they had left off when I entered and asked an older woman sitting only two seats away from me, to go on with what she was saying. This woman was probably in her early sixties, heavy set with medium length gray hair, and wearing navy blue sweat pants, a matching sweatshirt and light blue fluffy slippers. Since I came into the conversation in midstream, I wasn't quite sure what she was talking about. I kept my eyes in her general direction, but was feeling uncomfortable about being new to the group.

Just then, I begin to feel a flighty, great feeling zooming up in my brain. Now I didn't care what the old lady was talking about, nor who was in the room or what they were talking about. There was nothing better than the feeling I was experiencing at that exact moment. Whatever the doctor ordered, I was in total agreement and liked the early results. For the remainder of the group, I just soaked in my long awaited relief from reality, until I heard Keith begin to wrap up. He stated we had about an hour of free time to relax, make calls, watch TV, lie down or whatever we liked within the unit. Before he even had that information out of his mouth, the others were getting up and walking toward the door to exit.

Keith asked me to stay behind and I felt as though I had done something wrong. I reminded myself to look him in the eye and answer his questions with whatever would get me out of the situation comfortably. Although I was still a rookie with manipulation, it was on my mind and I was up for practicing.

Keith asked me to sit in an empty chair, and then shut the door and took a seat himself. *Oh man, this is not good.* I was afraid he was going to ask me why my eyes looked so foggy. I was just feeling the high and now someone was going to nark on me. I was surprised when Keith shared he wanted to take a moment to introduce himself and give me the opportunity to share any issues I may want to work on in this group.

Keith told me he was a group counselor and had been doing this for a few years. He was in his early thirties, with blond hair and a matching mustache, gold rim glasses, a slim build and a bright smile. In addition, Keith told me a bit about himself and his family and he looked in my eyes and smiled throughout most of the conversation. I felt he connected with me before he knew me.

When he stopped talking, I knew it was my turn and since I was feeling a pretty good buzz at the time, I decided to take a chance on this guy and shared information about my family and my medical situation. After telling him my story, I added I had become dependent on the meds a little bit, but felt I had a handle on the situation, even though my family disagreed. I was honest, didn't overplay and didn't manipulate. I trusted him, but also didn't want him to stand between me and my drugs. I made a note to myself to watch out for those I liked and trusted as they could be an enemy in disguise.

Now that I had used half of my morning break speaking with Keith, he stated I could go and do what I needed before the next activity. Keith added he would formally introduce me to the group that afternoon, give me an opportunity to share something about myself and give the others a chance to introduce themselves to me.

After Keith and I left the room together, he went to the nurses' station, while I went down the hallway leading to my room. Although I was feeling a good buzz, I was exhausted from sleeping only two hours. After showering, changing my clothes and lying down, the announcement came over the intercom that leisure group would start in five minutes and each of us was expected to participate and meet in the community room.

Leisure group? What the heck does that mean? I was utilizing leisure time by sleeping, what better leisure was there? Exhausted, I sat on the edge of the bed and took a second to get a current buzz barometer reading, which told me I could use more meds, but I would be okay for about an hour with the buzz I was enjoying. At least now, I did not have to worry about withdrawal. In fact, my buzz was stronger than before, or at least different. My hair was tingling; my heart calm, my body relaxed, the world was at peace and my mouth was dry. I was feeling good.

I threw on a baseball cap to cover my messy hair and walked into the community room where about twenty people were seated around the lunch tables. I saw Jerry's familiar and friendly face and walked over to sit by him. Jerry greeted me with a big, white smile and handshake. He asked me how things were going and if I had unloaded all my hang-ups and issues in therapy group. I just grinned and said it was interesting. I asked how his group went and he stated he had used every minute of his time to manipulate and persuade not only the others, but the counselor, into believing he was severely depressed and having a battle with suicidal thoughts.

Up to this point, I would not have believed anyone would want others to think they were sick, when they were healthier than a horse. However, I would find myself following in Jerry's tracks, acting out the same way, and finding myself to be a viable nominee for an Academy Award in the category of Best Actor.

Now that the 'prisoners' were gathered in the community room, a young woman came in and announced she was the leisure time facilitator and as a group, we were going to participate in a fun activity. *How much fun can we have on a rehab floor?* In a voice, much like a kindergarten teacher, she stated we were going to play indoor balloon volleyball. As I looked around the room, I saw about three fourths of the group roll their eyes and I heard several negative sighs of disapproval.

It was clear the facilitator was more excited about playing the game than we were. She attempted to win us over by inflating three or four different color balloons to the size of volleyball and then throwing them into the air in our direction. As the balloons sailed into the air and drifted toward the floor, there was only one person who tapped one balloon back into the air. The facilitator grabbed one balloon and proceeded to teach us the game we attempted to play for the next forty-five minutes. Thankfully, leisure time then ended. I did not enjoy participating in activities with people I didn't know, and in games better suited for children, especially when I was feeling sober. I was coming down from my morning high and felt frustrated, sore and tired. I was also feeling betrayed by my family for dumping me off with no warning. The young facilitator stated it was 11:45 and lunch would be at noon. Before then, we were to line up for the distribution of medications. That's all I needed to hear in order for me to get in the med line and start the spinning wheel of thoughts about what medications I would receive and what kind of high they would provide.

Standing second in line behind another man I recognized from my therapy group, I imagined just how great my next high would be. I focused on the relief it would bring from the physical pain and emotional stress. I also thought about the actual lightheaded feeling I loved, the sleepy effect a high provided and feeling as though I didn't have a care in the world. It would also get me through the afternoon's activities, which I was totally unprepared for. It would definitely assist me in introducing myself to the therapy group and getting through that awkward situation.

I provided the nurse my name, birth date and showed her my arm bracelet for identification. Before swallowing the pills, I recognized two out of the six. I didn't care what they were as long as they provided what I was looking for—the next ultimate high. I threw away the two small Dixie cups and walked back to the community room, where I grabbed the lunch tray with my name on it. I, once again, look for my friend and mentor, Jerry.

Jerry was sitting at the end of a table and smiling from ear to ear with a bright toothy grin. I didn't waste any time in sharing my manipulation tactics that were starting to make perfect sense to me. Jerry also shared I needed to watch everything I said in group and one-on-one appointments, because the doctor and counselor were paying attention to my every word and action. My actions and words would have to match what I wanted and needed.

After lunch, we had a thirty minute break and I went back to my room and lay down. The nurse then came in and told me it was time for me to meet with the psychiatrist. I felt a sudden rush of excitement knowing this was my opportunity to score more and better drugs, but I dreaded not knowing exactly what I was walking into.

How Did I Get Here?

I walked the short distance from my room to the psychiatrist's conference room, where he met with each patient individually. When I walked in, I realized it was the same doctor from the previous evening. As I sat in the chair, the doctor never acknowledged me. Just like my previous experience, he sat and looked over my file as if I wasn't there.

Several minutes later, the doctor looked up at me and asked how I was doing. I took my time answering his question.

"Not good," I said.

"What's going on?" he asked.

"I'm feeling frustrated, betrayed, severely depressed, tired beyond belief and my lower back is killing me with the sitting this unit requires," I said. "I'm feeling a bit paranoid about being with the others and being in a group is very hard for me."

The entire time I spoke, the doctor looked at his lap. When I finished speaking, he looked up for a brief moment.

"Do you feel like you want to hurt yourself?" he asked.

"Yes, I feel depressed at times." I put my hands on my head. "The pain is so bad; I just can't take it any longer."

"I've prescribed a new antidepressant for you," he said. "It should help with your anxiety. I'm also adding a new pain medication. " He stated he would look at my chart and make a decision about what he might add to assist me with the issues I was suffering from.

I told him how much I appreciated his help and as I walked out, I added I never thought life would take me down such a rough road. I was feeling pretty good about myself. I had taken Jerry's advice, played up the pain and misled the doctor to increase my chances of getting more or new pain meds. I played up the depression and suicidal thoughts, in order to get additional or new mood stabilizers. I was consistent, not overly emotional and stayed on point. Now, I just had to see how it worked out for me. I went from not understanding how Jerry could lie about his situation, to manipulating and lying about my own situation to get what I wanted—drugs!

Once again, the nurse told me group therapy was already in session and I could just tap on the door and walk in. I did as I was told and sat in the same chair in the small group room I had occupied earlier that morning. However, this time it was not the older woman speaking, it was a man about the same age as me speaking about his addiction to cocaine. While he was talking I kept thinking he was the real deal, an addict. The type who goes out and gets high, sells drugs, doesn't take a bath, lives under a bridge and quits school in the ninth or tenth grade. Feeling buzzed, I just stared at him as he spoke and felt a weird sort of respect for him. A man like him takes a risk and lives the high life, getting to experience a real high on real drugs.

After listening to this man talk about his addiction and how it had affected his life, Keith asked him some questions to help him think about how he could make steps in improving his life by working on a recovery plan. Keith told him the recovery plan would take plenty of hard work and self-discipline, but would be well worth the struggle and sacrifice. As they were wrapping up his focus time, I began to feel those familiar butterflies begin to fly around in my tummy again.

Just as I expected, Keith shared with the group there was a new member who joined that morning. My heart was pounding as if it was going to come out of my chest. I kept my eyes on Keith, as I was too nervous to look at anyone else. Keith asked me to share my first name, tell a little about myself, what brought me to this center, and what I would like to get out of this small group experience.

It was a good thing I was feeling a half way decent buzz at the time, but even with the buzz, I felt like a fish in a fishbowl.

"My name is Ken. I'm married and I have three small children," I said. "And I live in Muskegon." I shared how I was injured in an auto accident, a little about my back injury and surgery, and how I was having issues with depression and taking my prescriptions correctly. I relaxed a bit, looked around the room at the others as I spoke, and my heart began to calm down a little. Now, I only need to say what it was I wanted out of this group experience. I shared that since I had never been in a group like this, I wasn't sure what I needed or expected.

Keith thanked me for sharing and went on to tell me the rules of the group. There were many, but the one that stood out was that I was to respect others and what I heard in the group was to stay in the group. Keith then asked the others to introduce themselves and state what it was that brought them to the center. The man to my left began and they went around the room clockwise from there. I was realizing just how great these drugs were, because they made these kinds of situations easier to deal with. Feeling the effects of my drugs, whatever they were, made it almost enjoyable listening to the other prisoners and what it was they were charged with and what they were here for.

I found it interesting to hear I was not alone in dealing with certain issues, while others were dealing with things I had not experienced. Some of those issues were for drugs, alcohol, paranoia, depression, bipolar disorder, and suicidal thoughts. After the group members introduced themselves, Keith asked me to share more about what brought me here. The butterflies returned, but due to the drugs, I shared that I didn't feel like I belonged here, but my family felt I had a drug issue. I added that my family thought I had been acting strangely due to the drugs and they were worried I was getting worse. However, I needed the medications for the terrible pain I was experiencing from the accident, and my depression had become an issue due to my feeling like a failure as a husband and father.

I remember what Jerry had told me about watching what I said carefully and to stick to what I wanted and needed. I think what I had just told the group was consistent with what I had told the doctor and realized it was going to be a lot of work covering my tracks in order to get the one thing that would make my existence possible. However, the payoff would be great.

Keith thanked each of us for a great session, welcomed me as a new member, and added that he felt I would be a great addition to the group. He then excused us and as we left, Keith stated we had an hour break and then to gather in the community room for the next activity.

After group, I decided to call home to see how my family was doing without me. I was grateful to find no one was waiting to use the phone and I could walk right up and use it without standing in line. I punched in the number and heard the ring, feeling a bit nervous about what I was going to say. My wife answered and asked how I was doing. I stated I was fine, but I didn't fit in because these people had severe issues I didn't have. My wife, loving as always, told me I was in the right place and they could and would help me learn how to take my medications correctly, so I could live a productive and happy life.

"You don't understand," I said. "I am taking the medications correctly and I need them to deal with the pain and depression. I'm not an idiot and would never let drugs take control of me or my life.

"Your parents and I will be there tonight at 7pm to visit and we can talk about it more at that time," she said.

I was glad to hear I would be having visitors, as just seeing people would be good. We talked for about five more minutes and then ended the call knowing we would see each other in a few hours.

About forty five minutes later there was an announcement that all patients were to meet in the community room in five minutes. I closed my eyes to check my buzz barometer and decided it was on the low side. I could still feel a slight effect from the midday medications I took, but knew this part of the day would prove to be the hardest, since I had to make it to bedtime without taking anything. How was I going to do that?

As I walked into the community room, I saw most of the prisoners sitting there waiting for the next activity. Within minutes a middle-aged man came in and introduced himself as Rick. He informed us the next activity we would be doing was a craft activity. Oh great.

We followed Rick to the craft room I had seen the night before on the tour and it now looked a bit different. It was no longer empty and in order, as Rick had transformed it into a workshop that made me think of the North Pole where

Santa and his elves produced toys. The cabinets were now open and there were craft materials on every table and countertop. On the countertops were pieces of wood cut in different shapes, unfinished wood products, such as small wall shelves, key holders, napkin holders and several different wooden puzzles.

The large center table was covered with a clear plastic sheet where Rick had placed sheets of sand paper, paint sets, paint brushes, bowls of water for rinsing the brushes and anything else you might need to finish a wood craft project. He explained we were going to take a couple hours to relax and create a project we could take home. We could look around the room at the different selection of projects and choose what we wanted to work on individually. We were instructed to take our time, enjoy ourselves and if we had any questions, to just ask and he would be happy to assist us in any way.

Sitting there, I was not feeling a good buzz, as it had been a few hours since my last handful of pills and the great effect was beginning to wear off. If I had been at home, I would be opening one or two of the little orange bottles of pills, especially the ones with a sticker warning of side effects and instructions not to drive or use large equipment. I always looked for those warning stickers on my new prescriptions and finding them was like winning the lottery. How I would have loved to just take one of my own narcotic cocktails right then to help me relax and chill. As I was fantasizing about creating my own little high, Rick told me I could select a project and get started.

I selected a wooden train jigsaw puzzle and brought it back to my seat. Working on it for the next hour or so, I sanded each piece thoroughly. I stayed to myself, listening to some of the others talk and chat among themselves, but I didn't participate in any conversations. I thought about how I had disappointed my wife and family, yet they were coming to see me in a couple hours. Although I knew I was disappointing these precious people, I also knew I loved the feeling of getting high. The dilemma seemed so easy to fix by just not taking so many meds, but I didn't want to fix it at this time. What was wrong with me?

Once we were finished, I went back to my room and sat with my head in my hands. My back was killing me and I needed medications for both the pain and lack of a buzz. Sitting there, I felt alone and sad as it occurred to me once again I was letting others down and embarrassing my family. I was a Dutch-Reformed, grown man who was the son of a strict father and loving mother and I still ended up in this place. How did this happen? What did my wife and kids think of me? What did my parents think of me? What did my church think of me? Not to mention my fellow employees, my friends and my neighbors. I needed to find relief from these feelings and the only relief was in taking a handful of magic pills, my best and only friends at that point.

Love of My Life

After dinner, I walked back to my room feeling stiff and sore from the day's activities. Lying flat on my bed, I counted the dots in the ceiling tiles to keep my mind off the pain, both physical and mental. I must have fallen asleep, because the next thing I knew, a nurse was touching my arm to wake me up and telling me I had visitors. I felt a little anxious and thought about how a handful of meds would make this entire situation much easier to handle.

Before walking out of my room, I placed my hat on my head to cover my messy hair. I had to look good even in rehab, right? As I enter the community room, I see my wife and she stands and gives me a hug and kiss. I sit next to her and ask about the kids and she states they are fine, but they do wonder and question where I am. She says she has done her best to explain to them that I am at the hospital so the doctors can help me.

In the middle of our conversation, my thoughts go to my doctor's appointment the next morning. What would he ask me? What did I need to plan for? I wonder if there is any way I could manipulate him into giving me more meds. The meds he had given me thus far were giving me moments of what I wanted and needed, but it would be great if the buzz could last longer and be stronger. Just like an addict, I was chasing the bigger and better high.

"Ken?" my wife said.

"What did you say?"

"How did you sleep last night?"

"I only slept two hours, if that." I added that since I couldn't sleep, I had met a man in the community room and we watched television and chatted most of the night. Once again, my mind went from the conversation with my wife, to the fact I was running low on what it takes to provide an adequate buzz. I was hurting due to my back pain and feeling annoyed that I couldn't just take my meds when and where I wanted.

My wife's voice pulled me out of my little world and dragged me back to reality. However, I didn't have any idea what she was talking about, nor did I remember a thing about the present conversation we were having. My wife's facial expressions made it clear she was getting tired of having a one-sided conversation, with me gone half of the time.

"There's my son."

I looked up and saw my mom and dad walking toward me, smiling the entire time. I get up slow, due to the back pain and gave each of them a hug.

"So, is this place helping you?" my dad asked as we sat down.

"I'm not sure yet," I said. At that moment, I was thinking that what he wanted them to help me with and what I wanted were two very different things.

My mom's smile was gone from her face, as she stated she had nothing else on her mind but me ever since they dropped me off. My mother and I were close and had a special bond I never wanted to damage or break. She wiped at a tear running down her cheek.

My father, behaving as the politician he was, was speaking to my wife about unrelated issues and the weather.

After my mother and I stopped talking, my dad asked me what it was going to take to fix this issue and said he did not know what to do to help me this time. In the past, if I ever needed help with anything, I could always depend on my dad to be there for me. Although he never graduated from high school and quit after the eighth grade, he was smart and gifted. He had owned his own thriving business, ran for a political office, which he won and was re-elected to several times, then went on to be appointed to other offices as well. He could also figure out just about any math problem, fix anything, and had friends coming out of his ears, due to his kind and outgoing personality.

At that time, my dad noticed a room for smokers and with a smile on his face, told us he was going to have a quick smoke. I watched him enter the room, and even here in a rehabilitation unit, he said something to the three men sitting in there that made each of them smile. My dad was an amazing man I could only hope to be like.

With my dad gone, my mom and wife were talking about the kids and other family issues. Now, however, the attention and conversation turned to me. My mom asked how I was really doing and how I ended up here. My mom knew I was taking pain medications for the back surgery, but questioned why I was taking more medication than prescribed. My parents seldom took medications and couldn't understand people like me, who not only took medications, but took more than were prescribed and became addicted to those medications.

She did not understand how her youngest son had now found himself in the grips of addiction and in a rehabilitation center. Just then, my dad returned smelling like a Marlboro Red cigarette, sat back down and again stated he did not know what to do for me. I said I was sorry if I embarrassed my wife, parents or family by being here.

"Who gives a shit what others think," my dad said. "Just stay here and get the help you need and get yourself healthy, son."

I shared with my wife and parents that the doctor had prescribed new medications, never telling them he had simply added them to the list of present medications. I now was taking more prescribed medications than when I came in. We chatted for a while and when visiting hours were over, we shared hugs and kisses. As I watched them walk out together, I knew I was hurting and embarrassing them at the same time.

Those thoughts did not last long, as I turned my focus back to myself. My buzz had worn off and I was sore, anxious and frustrated. After watching my wife and parents walk down the hallway and exit through the locked doors, I sat back down on the chair and focused on the drugs I was going to receive soon and the high I would get from them.

With an hour of free time before group therapy to wrap up the night, I went to my room. With tears running down my face, I thought about the decisions I had made and how they had landed me here, dealing with a dangerous and deadly addiction problem and issues with depression. How could have I made all these bad choices and fallen into addiction? I knew I had a problem, putting pills before and above anyone or anything in my life. My thinking was messed up and taking these medications made me think I needed more and more of them, throwing me into a bottomless pit of addiction. My thinking had me making sick choices—like taking meds at wrong times, taking more than prescribed, and now learning how to manipulate doctors and health care professionals.

Still crying, I couldn't imagine how my kids were feeling. I had three beautiful children and here I was with a pill taking issue. Did I want them to grow up knowing and remembering their dad was an addict who cared more about drugs then he did about them? Right then, I heard the announcement for wrap up group. I wiped away my tears, not wanting anyone to know I had broken down and was beginning to realize how much pain I was causing with my actions and behaviors.

Soon, after the prisoners were accounted for in the therapy group, a staff member came in, shut the door and took a seat. She stated this was wrap-up group and we were asked to go around the room and share what went well and what we thought would be good ideas for us to work on tomorrow as individuals. As the first person who volunteered shared, all I focused on was what I was going to say when it was my turn. I had learned so much, however, I still had so much to learn and work on. I thought they would not want to hear what I actually wanted to work on tomorrow—to further my manipulation skills and build on using the doctor to get what I wanted.

After half listening to the others and their successes and goals, it was my turn. I shared my success for the day, making it through my first day. My goal for tomorrow was to work on how to repair and build relationships with family members and friends. As the next person began to share, I realized that after group I would get to take my meds for the night. I hated depending on others to give me my pills, but if I played my cards right, I might walk out of this place with more drugs than when I walked in.

Right about then, the staff member told us we were excused for the evening and to remember to line up for our medications at the regular time. Was she kidding? Did she think I would have to be reminded to line up for pills? It would only be twenty minutes before they would dispense medications, so I decided to be first in line and took a seat by the nurses' station.

Finally, a nurse began to hand out the pills and I was right there to take them. This time, although I did not have time to count them, I noticed there were more than last night and probably at least six or seven pills in the little Dixie cup.

Over the next twelve days, I watched, listened and learned how to be a better manipulator. By the time I was released from this facility, I had reeled in a gold mine of drugs. I not only manipulated the doctors and staff into increasing the doses of meds I came in with, I was successful in adding several new medications. While admitted to this ward, I said the things I needed to say and acted the part by keeping each and every story straight, in order to persuade the staff into doing things I thought I wanted and needed. Little did I know, the old saying of "be careful for what you wish for," would almost be my total demise.

Not (Always) A Quick Fix

Rehabilitation does not always go as one expects. I believe that is what my family was thinking not long after I arrived home from my first stint in rehab. Here I was at home and my original problem seemed to be worse. What they didn't know was that I had arrived at rehab not taking my meds as prescribed and now I had added several new meds. I was now high and intoxicated almost nonstop and at times, could even be found sitting in my chair, literally drooling on myself. If I was ever sober enough to think straight, I was researching my drug manual, as if it were a long awaited Christmas catalog and I was wishing for new magic pills, instead of the new and trendy toy.

After being home for close to two weeks and given somewhat free reign on the new meds I had been prescribed and was misusing, my family was not happy with the path I was taking. Therefore, it was decided I should return to the rehabilitation facility and almost two weeks later, I was readmitted to the same unit.

Looking back, my family had no experience with these issues and didn't know what type of rehabilitation unit to reach out to or to look for. In our prominent Dutch community, you never heard people talk about family members or loved ones being admitted to rehabilitation centers or talk openly about such issues.

During my second stay, I met a different doctor who was on staff when I was admitted. This doctor was in his mid to late sixties and looked even older. He was standoffish, unfriendly, never looked at me or made eye contact, and I picked up where I had left off from during my first visit. I used my new manipulation skills to make him believe that although I was taking a few too many medications, they were necessary for the terrible pain I was going through. I even had the guts to throw my family under the bus and say part of the problem was my family did not understand my situation.

He just sat in the same small conference room and appeared to not be interested in my situation. Most of the time, I questioned if he was even listening to me. But after the appointment was finished, I felt confident in my manipulation abilities and left the room feeling I did my best at asking for what I wanted: additional and stronger drugs. However, now the tables had turned a bit and I was dealing with a different doctor and a family disliking my new behaviors. Also, I had to work much harder at keeping my stories together due to the mental effects of the medications.

This rehabilitation visit went the same as the first—the schedule, groups, food, and my room, but I was able to add a few more medications. The added medications and their visible effects on me did not go over well with my family. They would come to visit and watch me stumble down the hallway and walk into walls, trying to keep my balance. I was slurring my speech, and having trouble keeping my eyes open and engaging in a sensible conversation. As the days went by, my family watched me deteriorate.

One day, I was called into the doctor's room for my regular morning appointment and found my mom and sister-in-law sitting in the room. I knew immediately something was up and it was probably not a good thing. They greeted me with smiles, but they seemed a bit indifferent.

The doctor asked what had brought them there and my sister-in-law took over the conversation. It took me by surprise as she was usually quiet and calm, but she was on a mission and it was obvious she did not like the plan of action the rehabilitation center had taken with my case. She could not get the words out fast enough and all I heard was "He is worse!" "He can barely walk without falling." "He can barely speak to us and carry on a normal conversation."

What was she doing? I had worked hard to ask for and get what I wanted and now my family was walking in and attempting to take it away. However, I did not know what to say either. I didn't want to take responsibility for asking for these meds in front of my family, but I also did not want to lose the pills. My sister-in-law called the doctor out on what he was doing and why he was doing it. The doctor, in his quiet and standoffish manner, shared he felt I was in need of the medications being prescribed, but he would look into the matter and reevaluate, if necessary. She asked for a time she could call him and see what he decided and he told her she could expect to hear something in the next day or two.

Later that day, I had just finished my afternoon therapy group and was sitting in the community room listening to my new cohorts talk. I was relaxing from the morning experience with my sister-in-law and my doctor, when I saw my dad walk around the corner. I was glad to see him, but he had a look about him I recognized as not good. Although a wonderful and personable man most of the time, my dad had a terrible temper. I could tell in an instant what kind of mood my father was in and this afternoon it was not a good one.

Before even saying hello to me, he walked up to the nurses' station and asked if his son Kenneth Start had been given his afternoon meds yet. They stated legally, they could not share that information with him.

"If you or anyone here gives my son one more damn pill, I will personally take it and shove it down your throat," my dad said. His voice was loud and exploded through the room.

Even in my mid-afternoon intoxication, I knew what I had just witnessed was real but not good. My dad walked a few feet away from the nurses' station, looked back at the nurse and gestured with his hand.

"Do you understand what I just said?" he said.

While the nurse stood there, my dad looked at me, waved and left from the same hallway he had entered.

You could have heard a pin drop in the entire unit. I even heard the door lock behind my dad as he left. At that moment, I felt as if I was ten again and my dad had just lost his temper and no one in his path knew what to do or say. My first thought was this could work out two different ways for me. The first result, not so good, was they would begin to see things the way my dad did and realize I probably don't need the medications they are prescribing. The second result, much more to my liking was their witnessing what kind of lunatics I grew up around would help them understand some of the mental pain I was explaining and living with. Once again, I was ready to throw my family under the bus for my own personal gain.

Now that my dad had left after such a great display of anger, and my mom and sister-in-law also attempted to blow my cover with my doctor, I went into addict survival mode. I once again heard Jerry's voice, "You have to know what you want and need and know how to ask for it." I knew what I wanted and needed and was beginning to gain the skills required to get just that.

Therefore, although shook up by my father's outburst and somewhat due to the effects of the medications I was taking, I continued on with my day. I ate dinner, had a few visitors, went to my evening wrap-up group, and played the entire incident up to what kind of family I was raised in which started a group discussion on family issues. Before I knew it, the focus had shifted from me and my family, to another individual in group, giving me time to regroup.

However, witnessing the pain I was causing my mom, sister-in-law and father, not to mention my wife, three children and others around me, was weighing on me. The weight was heavy, constant and at times, overwhelming.

It was this weight, along with the chronic back pain, that set me up for depression, a foe I would never wish on my worst enemy. Although my entire situation began with a car accident, which caused serious bodily injury and chronic pain and started a war with medications and addiction, I now found myself fighting new wars involving guilt, depression, growing addiction, manipulation, and suicidal thoughts.

Hell Disguised as Heaven

Now two years after my auto accident which started this downward spiral, I had undergone two back surgeries, and landed in and out of two rehab visits for the growing addiction to medications of mine, others and anything I could get my hands on. I had fallen in love with the high the medications offered me, the relief they provided from reality, and the false feeling everything was going to be okay. At this point, my life was Hell, disguised as Heaven.

My family had attempted to intervene twice with no success and I had warded off their attempts to help me as the drugs had become much more important. At this point, I had an appointment with a new psychiatrist whom we heard was good at dealing with individuals dealing with serious addiction issues. This appointment was about two weeks away and I had graduated to the point where I welcomed a new challenge to manipulate a doctor to my way of thinking. My success in manipulating the healthcare professionals at the rehabilitation center had given me a feeling that I had found something I was good at, willing to work at and ready to hone as a professional skill. However, I was now dealing with a large, ugly, and heavy demon on my back—depression, who also introduced me to his friends—guilt, shame, and suicide.

Dealing with a full blown addiction, severe depression, chronic pain and the things that came along with these terrible afflictions, I was a very sad individual. Before my accident and injury, I was a happy-go-lucky man with an outgoing and friendly demeanor. However, drugs and depression were stealing those personality traits away from me. I was now quiet, cold, manipulating and depressed.

With the aid of medications, I was beginning to see things not really there like bugs, rodents, rain in the house, and people, such as policemen, in my bedroom and other rooms in our home. I would be attempting to have a conversation with someone and see bugs, such as cockroaches, run up the individual's arm, to their shoulder and sneer at me while the individual talked. This was happening more and more with the increase of meds. I would also wake up in the middle of the night and see a policeman standing in the corner of the bedroom, as if he was standing guard. I would wake up my wife and ask her why there was a policeman standing in the corner of our room, only to learn he was not there, rather just a sick figment of my imagination and addiction.

Although I was experiencing several negative side effects from the increasing medications, the depression was by far the worst. The depression had become so severe, I was beginning to have suicidal thoughts, something I had never experienced before. I was feeling as though my life had been a complete failure; I would never find relief from the chronic back or emotional pain; God had turned his back on me; and, my life was no longer worth living. I was living in a black vortex.

The chronic pain, growing addiction and depression had spurred suicidal thoughts, which were speaking to me. I was having internal conversations with a feeling or thought, and was beginning to fight with a devil inside me. Every waking moment I found myself attempting to fight against this dark and deadly mental disorder.

Although I was fighting a war against this demon of suicide, I would also do just about anything to give it room in my life. I would sleep all day and stay up most of the night alone, giving it time to run through my head. I would spend time thinking negative thoughts, and by the time morning came, I had a horribly negative perspective of myself. I was surprised I made it through some of those tough nights alive without overdosing. My suicidal thoughts and addiction loved it when they got me alone and away from others. When I was alone, their power increased. When I was with others, my mind did not have as much control because my thoughts, as sick as they were, did not find confirmation. Alone with myself was when those sick, sad, unreal, and deadly thoughts were given the confirmation they needed to grow in my own head.

My mind never stopped, with thoughts going through my head faster and faster every waking moment. These thoughts misled me, spoke to me, and wanted nothing more than to kill me.

The faster the thoughts became, the weaker I got. I was giving the addiction and suicide the power, and the two demons were sucking the life right out of my physical and mental being. There were moments when I would get so wrapped up in negative thoughts racing through my mind at the speed of lightning, I would audibly cry out. At these moments, I would have to be alone, because I never wanted anyone around me to realize I was having these internal wars. I believed if I let others know I was having these issues, they would eliminate or change my medications. Then what would I do? Or rather, what would my addiction do? I had bought into addiction's lies and was feeding it everything it needed to grow.

Another interesting part of addiction and suicide I learned was that although I had the sense of control, in reality, I had given total control over to a false, manipulating thought and fleeting feeling. I bounced back and forth from feelings of total control, to moments of deadly surrender. One moment I was on top of the world, feeling I had just successfully manipulated a healthcare professional, family member, friend or entire situation; and the next, I was ready to end my own life due to a feeling and thought.

Adding to the sadness of this entire situation was the reality that I had been through rehabilitation twice but was now worse. How could I go into rehab and come out a sicker man? I took full responsibility for my part in that outcome, but I also questioned how some health care professionals could be scammed and manipulated so easily.

Trying to Escape

After coming home from the second rehab visit, my wife decided it might do the both of us some good to get a way for a short vacation. Together, we decided we would get a sitter for the three kids, which was no trouble with grandparents nearby, and spend three days in Northern Michigan, in the beautiful and relaxing city of Traverse City.

Although it was a cold and snowy winter in Michigan, Traverse City was one of our favorite places to get away. My wife made the sitter plans, hotel reservations and took a look at our budget to see what our limit would be for the weekend.

It was two nights before we were to leave and my wife and I were sitting in the living room watching TV together. The three children were tucked into bed and the house was quiet after another routine day of activity in our home. I had been attempting to watch my medication taking habits since I arrived home from the second visit of rehab. By that, I mean I was trying harder to keep my use from my family. They had become more involved in the last rehab visit and had learned, to some extent, that I was falling into the category of an addict.

Life had become just a bit more difficult for me now, or should I say, more of a challenge. I came home from the second rehab visit with new and stronger psychiatric medications, along with the same high dosage of pain medications I went in with. Now, I was once again researching these new medications with the thoroughness of a diamond inspector. I looked at every facet of the drug, every characteristic, every potential side effect and wanted to learn everything I could about it and so I did. I learned one of the new medications happened to be a controversial medication at the time. This medication had even been blamed for a woman mentally losing it and killing her husband in the state of Florida.

I had noticed a new and intensified feeling of being high since starting this med and fell in love with it. After I filled my little orange prescription bottles, I arrived home and added them to my current at-home pharmacy, where I found myself losing control of taking them as prescribed. I would use every opportunity to sneak these pills while no one was watching. My family had begun to see I was having addict tendencies, but they still were not wise to how an addict thinks, behaves and manipulates. My family members were not idiots, they just did not know anything about addiction and did not have the knowledge or expertise to know what to look for or expect. This was just what a blooming addict, like me, came to appreciate and expect.

My pill taking was out of control by now, and I had become so cocky I thought I could take anything and it would not hurt me. I wasn't a druggie out on the streets, I would never take too many, and I certainly would never overdose. I just loved the feeling they provided, so I took more and more to chase the next and bigger high.

That evening my wife was cross-stitching while we both watched television. Already feeling the effects of the several pills I had taken that day, I went into the bathroom and locked the door. I then quietly, I mean quietly, opened the door on the cabinet over the sink. I had to push on the edge of the mirror and it would pop open. However, this was an older model and it did have a faint squeak to it, and heaven forbid my wife would hear it. I softly opened the cabinet and there were my new favorite friends. My heart began to pound a few beats faster.

Just as quietly, I opened up the new bottle of pills and took three or four, not remembering how many I had taken earlier. I closed the bottle and put it back. Then I decided three or four was just not enough, so I opened the bottle again and took three or four more. Now my heart was jumping with excitement.

I closed the cabinet just as quietly as I opened it, used the restroom, washed my hands and went back out into the living room. I sat back down in my lazy boy chair and resumed watching television, as if nothing had just taken place. In my sick mind, I thought nothing had happened other than me successfully getting away with taking the perfect pills for the ultimate, perfect high. The excitement created by this ordeal was for the next high. I never thought for a second about what I had just done and the possible effects of my action. And I never thought about how my decision could affect those who care and love me.

“What were you doing in the bathroom, Ken?” my wife asked.

“Nothing.”

“What were you doing in the bathroom?”

Once again, I lied.

“How many pills did you take?”

“Why do you think I took any pills? Geez can’t a guy go to the bathroom?”

“What kind of pills did you take?”

“I didn’t take any pills.”

She started crying and stating she believed I had just taken pills while in the bathroom and felt I was putting pills before her and the kids. I had definitely put pills before her and the kids; I had put them before everything in my life.

I was moved to at least give in a bit and state yes, while in the bathroom I did take a few pills, but it was nothing for her to worry about. Right away she sat on the edge of her seat, put down the cross-stitch piece she was working on and asked me what I had taken and how much.

Once again, being Mr. Consistent, I lied.

"It was just a pain pill or two—that was it," I said.

"I don't believe you," she said. "You're lying to me."

I attempted to say something to put her at ease, but she stood and asked me one more time, what had I taken. I was a bit shocked. What had gotten into her and made her think I would lie about such a thing? It felt like my house of cards was falling in on me, so I told the truth.

"I took seven or eight pills, just so I can sleep through the night," I said.

The tone of my wife's voice lifted from quiet and controlled, to agitated and angry. "Why would you ever take so many?" she asked. "Taking that many, on top of what you just took a few hours ago, is going to add up in your blood stream and could cause your heart and other vital organs to stop while you're sleeping."

It might have been the shocked look on my face, but then she asked if it was only pain medications I had taken.

"No, none of the pills were pain medications," I said. "I took seven or eight of the new psychiatric medications I was sent home with from my last rehab visit."

My wife went into a calm panic mode, if there is such a thing, and asked if I realized what I had just done.

"Yes, I took seven to eight pills I had taken a liking to, due to their added effects."

My wife was crying and told me I had no idea what I was doing and she could not believe I was selfish enough to not even think of the children or her and just play Russian Roulette with my pills and my life. My wife's seriousness began to scare me and I began to think that maybe this time I had gone too far.

"What do you think I should do now?" I asked.

She wasn't sure, but thought I better get them out of my system as quick as possible.

Ten seconds later, I was in the bathroom vomiting up the pills I had just taken. Halfway through vomiting, I began vomiting through my nose. I swore right there, I would never find myself in this situation again; this had to be my new low point.

After that gross, pathetic and unforgettable moment, my wife and I went back out into the living room, not knowing what to do. My wife questioned if we should go to the Emergency Room to seek help with an overdose attempt. I thought it was not a big deal since I had thrown up the pills. All was good. However, I was upset I had just wasted seven or eight pills.

"I'm sick of not trusting you," she said. "It feels like those pills are more important than anything else in your life."

"You're being dramatic," I said. "I could quit anytime."

"Then quit," she said, challenging me.

"I don't want to."

"Ken, it's either the drugs or the kids and me," she said, without a tear in her eye. "The choice is yours, Ken," and you have to make it now, not later."

This was a predicament. What was I to do? I wanted my wife, kids and drugs. As I was thinking, the room was dead silent other than the sound of a Dateline episode on the television. Drugs or family, this couldn't be happening. Could I have one extra handful now to enjoy one last hurrah? What was I going to do? I had only been married six years and I was a drug addict. I couldn't let my wife down and I certainly couldn't give up my kids, so the decision that evening was, "I am done with the drugs."

I was not happy about being made to choose, so it was not the moment for a hug or anything like that. I marched into the bathroom, opened each of my little orange bottles and one by one, threw them in the toilet. When I finished with the bottles in the bathroom, I went into the kitchen and retrieved a couple of bottles and dumped them into the toilet. Seeing the different sizes, shapes and colors of my pills in the bottom of the toilet, was almost enough to make me grab them, but instead I flushed the toilet and watched them go down as the water washed them away.

I thought watching my pills swirling down the toilet was the hardest thing I had ever done, but I was wrong. My decision was hard, watching them disappear was harder, but the effects of stopping these drugs were by far the hardest.

I went to bed with mixed feelings. Part of me was proud of the fact I had made my wife happy with my decision and I had made a new start. However, another part of me was mad as hell that I had just wasted so many pills. Why didn't I just hide them and say I stopped? Why was I so weak and stupid to throw them away? What had I done? Two different lines of thought were running through my mind, one good and one deadly.

I was awake in bed for almost the entire night. If I had been alone, I would have screamed out in mental agony and utter pain. As the night went on, I would lie down and try to sleep, get up and walk around the house, attempt to watch television and go back to bed, just to start the same cycle over again. I fell asleep when the sun was just about to rise, with tears of confusion, desperation and regret.

What Is Happening to Me?

The car ride to Traverse City was quiet and a bit uncomfortable due to the lower back and left leg pain inflamed by the ride, and the fact I was mentally a wreck, due to giving up my meds thirty hours earlier. I had given up the one thing I believed was making me happy and giving me purpose in life. I could not get the drugs out of my head. I felt different physically and mentally without them, like I had just walked away and ended relationships with some of my best friends.

My wife had taken the driving responsibilities since I had not driven in over four months, due to not being mentally alert enough because of the drugs. As we drove, I found it hard to find things to talk about. I had nothing on my mind other than the drugs and how I was going to survive without them. My wife attempted to start conversations about different topics, but my mind and heart were not on the same page and I was not in any mood to just agree, as if everything was hunky dory.

This trip was not like the countless trips we had taken before my accident. Those had been full of fun and relaxation; this trip had an entire different purpose and feeling behind it. The purpose was to get me away from the house, kids, life, pain and the sadness, just for a few days. The truth was that no matter where you go, your problems follow you. Especially when the problems are nestled physically, spiritually and mentally within yourself.

After arriving in Traverse City, we checked into our favorite hotel on the bay. I agreed to do whatever she wanted and we drove the short distance to the mall. After walking through the mall, sitting and watching people, as my wife shopped, we grabbed a light bite to eat in the large food court and decided to stop at another large retail center on the way back to the hotel. After getting through the retail center pretty quickly, due to my increased back and leg pain, we drove back to the hotel where we rested a bit. I was now in terrible pain and didn't know what to do. I had no narcotics, muscle relaxers, opiates, psychiatric meds or anything. I would have done anything for something to knock me out so I could sleep through some of the misery. My wife gave me three or four tablets of ibuprofen, but I might as well have taken a handful of candy.

As my wife sat on the bed and cross-stitched, I laid next to her and tried to rest, but my mind ramped up and was going nonstop, thinking about the drugs and what they could do to help me at that moment. I was angry with myself for volunteering to not only give them up, but for flushing them down the toilet. What kind of friend would do such a thing? I had flushed them like it was nothing. What had I done? The more I thought about it, the more frustrated and agitated I became.

I found myself missing the bottles themselves and knowing they contained everything I needed. It was a form of security for me and now it was gone. I didn't have the bottles, the pills, the comfort, the high or the relief they provided.

That evening we went to dinner at one of our favorite steak houses and the next day we walked downtown together. Traverse City is a beautiful town and still had an old town charm with old downtown roads, sidewalks, structures and buildings one remembers as a child. People window shopped popular clothing stores, locally owned pharmacies, theaters, restaurants, ice cream stores, specialty shops, hobby stores and the like. Although it was cold and blanketed with an inch or two of fresh snow, there were plenty of people walking through town that day, but my mind was on only one individual—me.

I could not break away from the mental pain I was experiencing and I started feeling sick as if I was coming down with the flu—stomach ache, sweats one moment and chills the next, headache, tremors, lack of energy and a bit nausea. Although these symptoms were slight, they made my trip a little harder to enjoy. I didn't tell my wife about the symptoms, fearing I would wreck the weekend for her. I pushed on and looked forward to getting back to our room and lying down.

After an active day of shopping, eating and sightseeing, we returned to the room and I was whipped. I was tired, sore and my flu symptoms had ramped up a level. In the morning, after a rough night, I felt better, but the flu-like symptoms were still present. We went to the lobby of the hotel and she ate breakfast, but I did not want anything to do with food at this point and even the smell of food was a bit nauseating.

After breakfast, we checked out and took a ride to the Leelanau Peninsula, another beautiful and scenic part of the Traverse Bay area. I wasn't much company for my wife, as I would drift into a nap and then hear my wife say something or hear the radio and wake for a few minutes, only to slip back into a light sleep. By early afternoon, we arrived at the Leelanau Peninsula, looked at some of the beautiful winter scenes, then headed back to Traverse City for dinner and then home.

While in Traverse City, my energy level dropped, the tremors became worse, the nausea continued and I was going from cold to actually having sweat run down my back in seconds. Not to mention, every second I was still thinking about the drugs I had given up. What had I done? What was I going to do? The pain level had increased and I felt like crap.

I was anxious to head home, so we decided to stop at a fast food joint instead of a nice sit down restaurant. While my wife waited for the order, I sat at a table in the lobby. By the time my wife got our order and drinks from the self-serve soda fountain, I had taken a nose dive.

I felt as though I was freezing and was shaking uncontrollably. I tried to use my hands to open the burger wrapper or hold the burger itself, and I couldn't. I started to panic. What was going on? I didn't want the food, couldn't serve myself, felt as though I was going to vomit any second, and the muscles in my legs and arms began to ache. My mouth was dry, my head hurt and felt like it was going to pop off my shoulders at any time, and I felt like my life might be coming to an end. I had never felt this terrible in my life. Was I having a heart attack, a stroke, an aneurism? I didn't know, but whatever it was, it was not good.

By now my wife was beginning to feel a bit nervous, as well. When I could not use my hands to open and hold the sandwich, her eyes filled with worry and panic. She took a few bites of her meal and said she was going to bring me to the local emergency room. I didn't want to go the hospital in Traverse City; I just wanted to get in the car and head home. If I was going to die, I wanted to die at home or at least in a hospital in Muskegon. After a somewhat heated conversation, my wife finally agreed to honor my wishes and we headed for home. Usually a speed limit driver, my wife drove faster and seemed nervous the entire trip. About halfway home, she asked me to please let her take me into the emergency room there. Again I said no. She kept driving, making it home in good time and I was never so glad to see my own bed.

I was now a complete mess and just wanted to be left alone. I would go from the bedroom to the bathroom; finally just staying in the bathroom for several hours. I would lie on the floor wrapped up in a blanket, and then place a cold damp cloth on my head. One minute I would be puking in the bath tub, the next sitting on the toilet with severe diarrhea. On top of this, my muscles throughout my body were aching and throwing fits that felt like Charlie horses. My large motor skills, such as using my hands, were messed up, and my arms and hands were shaking and aching to the point I was not able to use them to do normal tasks. I sat on the linoleum floor in the bathroom, feeling the coolness of the floor and wondering if I was going to die.

The next morning, my wife called our doctor and he related that I was in withdrawal from the medications. He told her the withdrawal could be severe, but it would not kill me. It could last several days to weeks, but the symptoms should lessen in a few days.

What was I thinking? I quit all my medications to feel this sick? I could not believe what I had done; and I wanted my medications back. However, I had thrown them down the toilet and right now, I was in no shape to go to the doctor and ask for more. Nor was I in any shape to go to a family member or friend's home in order to hunt for any drugs I could steal. The most severe portion of withdrawal went on for the next five to six days, but the steady withdrawal went on for weeks.

My dad was being sworn into office as county commissioner a week after this started and wanted me there, sick or not. I didn't want to disappoint him so I went, but I had to wear a winter jacket with large pockets so I could place my hands in the pockets to cover up the involuntary jerks and severe tics. I was so self-conscious about how ridiculous I looked: pale, sick, aching, nauseous, hands jerking uncontrollably, eyes deep set with dark circles. I didn't look like a son my father could be proud to have by his side. However, my dad was glad I was there and I was thankful I did not miss my father's moment of achievement and honor.

Withdrawal sucked and I had never been so sick. I was fighting a battle between not wanting to use again, due to the withdrawal experience, and wanting nothing more than to swallow a handful of magic pills which would make the pain and suffering go away within minutes. My mind would be settled one moment thinking nothing good would come from taking these pills, to the next moment of wanting to run back to the pills and the wonderful relief they provided from everything. This was a battle an addict fought every moment of the day—knowing what was right and what we should do, but throwing it all to the wind for what felt good.

Some of the symptoms improved, but I did not feel like myself for the following two weeks. Other than attending my dad's swearing-in ceremony, I sat around the house sick, depressed, filled with anxiety and for much of the time, wanting nothing more than to steal, lie, cheat or manipulate someone so I could get more meds. My time was pure hell. I needed help to either get what I needed, which was professional help, or help to get the drugs I wanted.

I Can't (or Won't?) Hold On

Although I had experienced these terrible effects of withdrawal and had been sicker than I had ever been, it wasn't enough to come between me and my first love—medications. I worked hard at staying clean for close to two weeks, but could not hold on and ended up taking pills from individuals close to me. It was enough to get a buzz here and there, but not enough to stay buzzed.

I manipulated my schedule, visits and behaviors just enough to get me where I needed to be to get what I wanted. Although I did not score as much as I wanted, I did get enough to keep me somewhat in a haze.

Desperation had me doing things I thought were never possible. I would have never stolen from family members, friends, acquaintances or anyone. However, now I would do anything to get what I wanted, when I wanted it. I allowed my behaviors to be determined by an illness.

At this point, I was getting enough pills to keep myself in a mild to moderate buzz most of the time and was warding off the terrible monster called withdrawal. In this time period, my family physician and wife had set up an appointment with a psychiatrist, who was known to be one of the best in our area, for working with people who had behavior issues.

This appointment was either going to be just another notch in my belt or a time of change for me.

I was looking forward to the challenge and also looking forward to rebuilding my stock of little orange pill bottles. I knew the psychiatrist could prescribe some potent meds and that was what I was in need of. I had planned out what pills I would ask for in my own subtle little way.

My run-in with withdrawal was not enough to stop the addict in me and I was ready for round two. Addiction had me willing to do anything in order to get what I wanted or until it had me six feet under.

I went to the doctor's office looking forward to the new challenge of getting what I wanted and left with a new plan altogether. You see, the doctor was ready for me. In his experience, he had seen me or shall I say others just like me, over and over again. I thought I was unique, one-of-a-kind or special, but in reality, there were many people just like me dealing and coping with the disease of addiction. He was prepared for my attitudes, manipulation skills, display of emotions and excuses. He had been down this road and made it clear right from the beginning of our first appointment. He was not there to be messed with and if I was not interested in recovery, this was the time to leave and he pointed toward the door.

I was a bit taken aback to say the least. I had not run into a doctor like this and I was not prepared for his type—the type who wanted to help get you physically and mentally healthy. I was not sure if I was ready for that and I know my disease was not. Throughout the appointment, I had an internal war going on. On one side I wanted to give in and reach out to him for help. The other side was telling me to get up and walk out, I could do this on my own and there were plenty of other doctors willing to get me what I needed. I just had to get up, walk out and look for another doctor, a better doctor.

My addict mind worked all the time and was selfish, manipulative and didn't care who it hurt, as long as it got what it wanted. I compared it to a toddler who would cry if they didn't get what they wanted and cried until they got it. Addicts do the same thing—cry, fuss and moan until we get what we want. Even if what we want is the one thing that will kill us.

After listening to what the psychiatrist had to say and going through my own battle of tug-of-war between recovery and addiction, I decided I would take his offer of help and see if I could beat the disease. I wanted to become the man I once was and the man my family needed me to be. I left agreeing to give up using and call him if I felt I was in a bad place and needed to get something.

Before I left, he gave me a prescription for a non-addictive anti-depressant. So I went home with a little orange bottle, but this one had the goal of getting me better. Also before leaving, the doctor told me that the first time I did not follow his rules I would be released from his care.

The next eight months, I worked together him on a regular schedule with some serious talks, and began to take baby steps into recovery. I even began to feel a bit better about myself. He had given me a path to follow and with each step, I felt as though I could see a light at the end of the tunnel. Addiction did not want to give me up easily though and I still struggled with urges to use and go back to that way of life.

What felt the best during those eight months was that I began to feel better, clearer, and more present, more like the Ken I once knew and liked. I was still experiencing severe back and leg pain, but was following his advice to walk a bit and I did find some relief from the pain by being more active. I would walk around the neighborhood, or take my toddler daughter to our local mall and push her around several laps a day. I went back to church, community events, family functions and other activities I had given up since my surgery and fight with addiction.

Addiction was always on my mind tempting me and trying to make a case for how much better life would be with the medications and drugs, but with the help of the doctor, my recovery, exercise routine, family and for the most part, a positive attitude, I was able to ward off the temptations and stay clean. I was also feeling better taking the anti-depressant the way it was prescribed, which was new for me. My suicidal thoughts had become a lot better, although I still found myself feeling low, but now I had new ways of coping with the depression in order to avoid getting to the very low point.

My doctor taught me how to reach out to others on a regular basis, instead of just when I needed it. He also showed me how to slow down the negative thoughts and replace them with things like exercise, reading or other activities to change my focus. Most importantly, I was meeting with him on a regular basis, sharing my thoughts and feelings, and having him reiterate them. By him doing so, I learned how ridiculous some of my thoughts, feelings and beliefs had become.

In the eight months I worked with him, I began to not only think of him as a doctor but as a friend. I worked hard to change my life and looked forward to our meetings. Each time, I left with a sense of hope and energy. I respected him and he in return, treated me with respect and dignity. He believed in me and had expectations for me to succeed.

However, he was offered a new position on the east coast, and left to start this position within weeks of telling me.

Not Yet Willing

I had worked hard, listened to my doctor, followed his instructions; white knuckled it at times, went through hell to find some recovery and now was alone with my good old friend, addiction. What was I to do? Addiction was an old friend I was comfortable with, addiction knew what I needed, knew me inside and out, cared about me and would help me relieve my mental and physical pain.

My doctor had set up an appointment for me with another psychiatrist before he left and I followed through with the appointment. I even attempted to follow through with what my doctor had taught me during the eight months I had found success. However, within two or three weeks I was back to my old behaviors of lying, manipulating and stealing in order to find, get and take the pills which would relieve the pain and misery I thought I could not handle. After all that work, I found myself giving in within a short period of time.

At this point, I was still having immense lower back and left leg pain. I was seeing my orthopedic surgeon about once every six months and he would take a new x-ray to make sure things were progressing. He would also evaluate my medication regiment, or rather the list I shared with him. However, he was not stupid and had kept track of me through rehabilitation units. He had done his research and knew I was not one to be trusted with medications, nor was I being honest or open with what I was actually taking.

He even showed up without warning at one of my rehabilitation visits, and had a heart-to-heart talk with me about my situation and poor decision making skills. He tried his best to convince me to listen to the medical professionals in the unit and get my life together. Then he offered his assistance and told me he was willing to help in any way he could.

As time went on and my pain did not improve, even with the use of prescribed medications, exercise or physical therapy, the orthopedic surgeon was not sure how to proceed. At my next scheduled office appointment, he told me he felt bad there was nothing more he could do for me. He felt with my chronic pain, addiction, depression and suicidal thoughts, I needed to follow through with a mental health professional on a regular basis. He believed I needed to apply for Social Security Disability Benefits, feeling I would not be able to return to work with the permanent injuries I had received. I did not fully understand what the benefits were, but I would look into them in order to provide for my wife and children.

During the appointment, he also shared he had heard of a physician who was working with internal morphine pumps and a pump might be an option for me due to my addiction issues and behaviors. I could not control the level of medications being distributed through the pump as it could only be controlled and calibrated by a licensed and trained surgeon.

I followed his advice, or should I say, I sort of followed his advice. I tried non-addictive meds, even though I thought they were a waste since they did not provide the potent high feeling I loved. I met with the mental health professional, but only to get what I wanted out of the situation. I also took the information about the internal pump surgeon and made an appointment with him.

Applying for Social Security benefits was another issue I had to deal with. I was brought up in a family which believed you had to earn a living, work for things, and not depend on others or the government. So applying for disability benefits was a humbling experience, to say the least. I had worked hard for what I had since I was a kid and this was admitting defeat.

I had been attending the local community college at the time of my accident, taking general education classes in order to receive my Associate degree in arts. I then wanted to go on and earn my Bachelor's degree and receive my teaching degree. So I decided to go back to school. What made me think I could take on college classes? I signed up and planned to start college, but addiction had other plans for me and I would have to put my college plans on hold.

My anxiety and depression were now taking larger pieces of my mind and time. And I was allowing it to take me to new lows. The depression and anxiety were now so severe; the suicidal thoughts were constantly telling me I had nothing to live for. I had become a drug addict who lived in chronic pain and was now good for nothing. I had started thinking about how I would commit suicide and had come up with a complete plan.

It was the night before the planned suicide attempt and my beautiful family was having our family pictures taken. I was about to have my family pictures taken and I was higher than a kite, thinking it was going to be my last night with them and the last night of my life. This picture we were now sitting for would be the last image and photo they had of me, their young father.

After the pictures and a quick stop to have ice cream, we went home, put the children to bed and kissed them goodnight. That's when I made the mistake of taking too many pills in order to mentally handle my decision of taking my life. My wife noticed my situation and I ended up in another rehabilitation unit; this time, it was in a hospital located in a nearby city.

Addiction had taken me to a new low and its plans were to take me even lower. Now I found myself higher than a kite and in a new rehab unit. I had been taking so many meds at this time, later I wouldn't have many memories from this rehab visit which lasted just over a week. I went home back on track with my medications adjusted to what I was supposed to be taking and two new meds I had scored for pain.

I was home for just four or five days and things went bad once again. I had manipulated my way into another mess and almost overdosed. Now I was back in the rehab unit again and this time, I was there almost two weeks. This rehab unit was the same as the first in looks, schedule, group and individual counseling, food, and the all-important community room.

The community room was the most important room to me. I would talk and listen to others and learn things about addiction I never knew. I learned what others were doing to score drugs in places where people never thought possible and using drugs in ways other than swallowing and drinking them. I would make mental notes and keep these things tucked away in my sick mind, until I was free and able to research how I could benefit from these little tidbits—and benefit I did. I left this rehab visit not yet willing or ready to give up my best buddies and the great feeling of relief they provided.

This was my life with addiction where I was always looking for the one thing that wanted me dead. I was living in pain, sadness, sickness, self-doubt, depression and anxiety. I was manipulating just about everybody I ran into: medical professionals, friends and family. I continued down this road, living a life searching for the next and better high.

Chasing a Bigger and Better High

I was now living in a constant high, sometimes just enough to get me through the day and other times, knocked out and sleeping in bed. I was using the meds I scored from doctors, psychiatrists, hospitals, emergency rooms, as well as stealing anything I could get my hands on. Sometimes, it was obvious I was using because my personality was different than usual; other times, it was more difficult to tell and if you didn't know me well, you probably would not be able to tell.

It was during this time that, I followed up with the surgeon who was implanting the internal morphine pumps for pain relief. After my first appointment, the doctor felt I was a strong candidate for this surgery and would benefit from the pump with its time released of morphine entering my spine. I was scheduled for surgery and before I knew it, I had an internal morphine pump in the right side of my abdomen.

About a week after having this pump placed in my abdomen, the surgical scar became infected with staph and I had to have the complete pump, along with its catheters, removed. This was a tough thing to go through as I had been thinking the pump would be the answer to my prayers because it would deliver morphine right into my system and now it was gone.

I had done my research and knew morphine was a strong addition to my medication regimen and felt it could only help me find the next great high I was looking for.

The surgeon related to my wife that after I healed for about six months and was totally free of the staph infection, he would consider placing a pump into the opposite side of my abdomen. Upon hearing this news, I set my sights on the future. After getting out of the hospital, I was trapped at home due to an open wound the size of a softball in my abdomen. The surgeon could not stitch up the wound due to the infection that had to heal from the inside out.

It was during that time I decided I had to get my college education at whatever cost. I contacted the local college, made an appointment with an admissions counselor, spoke with financial aid and signed up for classes. Most of this I did over the phone, although I did have to go in to see the admissions counselor and financial aid department.

After speaking with the counselor, I decided to work toward my Associate's in Arts and then transfer to a four year college to finish a Bachelor's Degree. At that time, I did not know where my education was going to take me or what assistance it would offer me in my future. However, three months later, pretty well recovered from the staph infection, I found myself taking college classes at the local community college. What surprised me was how well I did in college. Before my accident, I was an A-B student, however now I had improved my grade point average and was earning only A's.

I was also no longer homebound, which left me able to find whatever pills and meds I needed to keep me at my desired high.

Six months after the first failed morphine pump attempt, the surgeon felt I was at a point where it would be safe to place a new pump in the opposite abdomen. I was all for it and willing to do it as soon as possible.

It was at this time I realized I was becoming addicted to surgeries. Maybe not to the surgeries, but to the medications they used to put you to sleep. I had fallen in love with the feeling of losing consciousness when they asked me to count backwards from 10 to zero. I had even fallen in love with just having them insert the IV.

The surgery was scheduled and it was a success. Soon afterward, I was on a regular schedule of having the pump checked and refilled. I would go to the pain clinic in the hospital to have the pump filled and calibrated, thinking the more I could get them to put in, the better I would feel. I went to each appointment ready to manipulate the surgeon into turning the pump up.

The refills were by far the worst part of the whole deal. They used a plastic template, which matched the size of my pump, and would feel my abdomen for the pump. Once they found a recognizable part of it with their fingers they would lay the matching template over my skin. The template had a hole in it about the size of a pencil eraser and they would jab a large syringe needle through the hole, hoping to find and break through the port located on the pump. This allowed them to refill it with the morphine. Most of the time, the staff would have to attempt to find the port ten or more times, which was a terrible experience and one I would not wish on anybody.

I was sick with flu-like symptoms from the pump; however, I was scared to say anything to anyone because that would mean possibly turning down the medication, changing the medication or even losing the pump altogether. I kept my mouth shut and put up with the refill experiences and sick feeling I was experiencing.

The sick feelings and symptoms would get worse the closer I got to the time for a refill; however, I was also taking meds the doctor never knew about. I didn't know how they were mixing with the morphine itself and the meds I took changed from time to time, depending on what pills I would obtain from new doctors, emergency rooms or steal from people in their homes.

Of course, the real goal of the pump was for pain management, but I was so lost in and controlled by my addiction, I never cared about the pain as much as the next and better high. Was the pump helpful for the pain? Who knew or cared? I just wanted to be high and I felt the pump was an easy way to build on my narcotic arsenal. My pain had become secondary. I just used my pain level to get what I wanted and it almost cost me everything, including my life.

A New Challenge

As luck would have it, my neighbor had asked me how I was doing. With a fake smile on my face, I stated all was good. My neighbor, seeing through me, asked me how things were really doing and I told him that I was struggling. I then shared with him the painful pokes it took to refill the pump, and the awful flu-like side effects.

He told me that his father, who resided in Florida for the winters had a similar pump, had a doctor there he spoke of highly. He also stated that his pump had been nothing but a miracle.

As the conversation continued, I became more interested in this doctor. My neighbor's father had none of the negative side effects I was experiencing and no horrible refill stories. I asked my neighbor if he would get me some information about this doctor, including a phone number and address.

Just over an hour later, he was knocking at my door with the requested information. After a short conversation he left and I went right to the computer to do learn more about this doctor and clinic.

I did a little research, but with the knowledge that this doctor could assist me with the negative side effects and painful refills, not to mention increases in morphine, I was excited to travel to Orlando, Florida where he was located.

Within two days I had called, made an appointment,

and was putting together plans for the trip. When it came to improving my medication situation, I was willing to jump through any hoop or drive anywhere to get what I wanted and needed.

Three weeks later, I was in sitting in the clinic's waiting room for my first appointment with the pain management doctor. I focused on the endless possibilities this appointment held for me and my personal situation. I also thought about just how far I had come to use my manipulation skills in order to increase my morphine levels. I had just flown from Michigan to Florida, and in my addict mind I believed I had graduated to the big league.

After what seemed like forever, my name was called over the intercom and a nurse stood by the examination entrance door with a chart in her hand. With a bright smile, she led me through two sets of doors and into a large room that resembled an emergency room. On one end was a large nurses' station surrounded by beds. These were separated with curtains to create makeshift private rooms. I was led into one of these rooms, asked to disrobe and handed a hospital examination robe.

Minutes later the doctor entered the room. Right from the start he was warm, friendly, genuine and caring. He got right to the point of my appointment and asked me about my injury and my experience with my pump up to this point. He also stated that he was surprised I would come all the way from Michigan to see him. I went into manipulation mode and began this relationship with my needs and wants at the top of the list, all the while pretending to be a patient in desperate need of help.

I was honest about my problems with the pump, the nausea, the chills and other negative side effects. In addition, I told him about the numerous painful experiences of refilling the pump, and that every unsuccessful attempt included a long, sharp silver syringe which inflicted pain. That's where my honesty stopped.

I exaggerated the pain level and told him the amount of morphine I was receiving was not near enough to cover the pain I lived with on a daily basis. I did have pain, but I was so tied up in the addiction and getting more morphine and other meds, I didn't even consider the true level of pain any longer. I just wanted more and I stuck to the story that the levels were never enough.

My story worked and I started a routine of travelling to visit this pain management specialist every three months for years to come. He not only made my refills an easier, more comfortable and more precise experience, I was able to use him to increase medications, first morphine and then Dilaudid. To my sick addict mind, this relationship was a match made in heaven. However, once again, it proved to be Hell disguised as Heaven.

During the years I went to Orlando, Florida to have my pump refilled, turned up and recalibrated, I met other pain specialists, surgeons and medical professionals. After six or seven years of working with these specialists and having continual issues with the flu-like side effects of my pump, even after switching from morphine to Dilaudid, it was suggested that I meet with a surgeon implanting spinal cord stimulators. A spinal cord stimulator would be surgically placed in the abdomen and would send electrical currents through the spine via electrodes inserted into the spinal cord. For me it would be in the opposite side as the existing internal pump, and would have a remote control. I could control the level of intensity the stimulator delivered and supplied to the spine to help control the pain. I was intrigued, interested and thought the stimulator would be great for pain, but not for the addiction.

However, as soon as I heard surgery I knew there was a lot at stake. As an addict, I loved the feeling of receiving anesthesia for surgery. Just the thought of hearing an anesthesiologist say those magic words, "Count from ten backwards," was exciting.

This put me at a crossroads. The surgery could alleviate some of my back pain, if not all. However, the doctors may also decide I no longer needed the internal pump that was delivering a dosage of strong medications on a constant basis. That would not be good.

Should I go through with the surgery, enjoy the deep sleep, high surgery supplies, and additional prescribed pain meds for recovery? Should I say no and continue with the medication regiment, manipulating and abusing drugs to get by? How could I, the addict, gain the most from this?

I decided to schedule an appointment with the surgeon to discuss the spinal cord stimulator. However, I would carefully prepare for this appointment by researching the stimulator and asking questions manipulatively to make the choice so I would get the best result and best return for my addiction.

Depression Wanted Me Alone

As I waited for my appointment with the surgeon, I was more nervous than usual as my wife and mother had come along on the trip. I would have rather walked into that office and examination room alone. I was good at manipulating, but meeting a new surgeon, talking about my pain situation, learning more about the spinal cord stimulator, and knowing the surgeon's goals and my goals for this surgery were two worlds apart, worried me. This appointment and first impression had to go my way and working alone had proven to work best for me.

Working alone this time was not going to happen; my wife and mother were accompanying me. The doctor was an older gentleman with white hair, wire rim glasses and a white jacket. He came in, asked a few questions, and had me lay back on the examination table while he felt my stomach and abdomen for my existing pump and also the other side, where I had the failed pump attempt and infection years earlier. After normal medical questions, he began to ask about my pain levels.

I shared with him that although I was under the care of a pain management specialist, I was still having a good deal of lower back pain and numbness in my left leg, which the pain specialist thought the stimulator would assist me with. The doctor then explained how the stimulator worked and how they would have to do a three day trial with the stimulator to see if it would be helpful for me, before actually surgically implanting it permanently. This meant two surgeries, offering me the chance to enjoy two great highs.

This appointment was going better than expected, as he shared he thought I was a good candidate for the stimulator. He felt he could do the trial surgery this trip and never spoke once about turning my pump down or off, which was what I was most concerned about. I thought for sure either this surgeon or my pain specialist would state that with the stimulator, I would no longer need the strong medications being released through the pump. However, nothing had even been mentioned about turning the pump down or off.

After the first surgery, to implant a three day trial stimulator, I stayed with my friends in the Orlando area for a few days, had a follow up appointment and then about a month later, flew back to Orlando to have my permanent stimulator surgically implanted. I now had an internal pain pump in one side of my abdomen and a spinal cord stimulator in the other, making me feel like the Six Million Dollar Man from the hit TV series in the seventies.

The spinal stimulator was a great help for the pain. I used it on a regular basis and enjoyed the relief it brought from the tiring and exhausting back pain. I would use the remote control that looked much like a TV remote, to turn the intensity of the stimulator up or down. In the beginning I would turn the intensity setting to a low/medium setting, but within only six months I was turning it up further and leaving it on most of the day.

During the time I was using the stimulator, I was still in full blown addiction. I was traveling from Michigan to Florida every three months to have my internal pump refilled, taking large doses of pain and psychiatric medications from a number of local doctors and hospital emergency rooms, as well as taking what I could from friends, family and anyone who unknowingly allowed me access of any type to their medications. Access meant pill dispensers or bottles on kitchen or bathroom counters; pills in bathroom cabinets, closets, or cupboards; pills in purses, cars, desks or anywhere else I could find them; and yes, I did find them. Most people didn't even realize medications setting out or in accessible places, were tempting to people battling addiction.

It was at this time I was awarded Social Security Disability Benefits for my injury and conditions. The benefits allowed my family to survive on a somewhat normal basis.

It was also during this time, with the pump and stimulator both implanted, I graduated from the local community college with honors. I then applied and was accepted for my under graduate degree at a four year institution, only forty five miles from my house. By the time I graduated from the community college, I had decided a degree in Business Management would work best as I had heard learning it would offer more options after graduation.

The college I decided to attend was one that matched my Christian faith. Although I was in full blown addiction, my faith in God was still there, although an active faith was another question. To make matters even more interesting, I decided to earn a Bachelor's of Science degree in Business Management, with an emphasis in Ministry Leadership. What was I thinking?

I attended this college for two years and graduated receiving my Bachelor's Degree with honors. It was an accelerated program that met once a week with the same group of cohorts over the two year period, just changing subjects and instructors. Throughout my educational experience there, the lowest grade I ever received was an A- and I was not happy about it. The classes were tough and I had to credit my hard work ethic for my success, even under the influence. I attended classes with many wonderful individuals and was fortunate enough to even meet up with two great ladies from my home town, affording us the opportunity to have study groups on a regular basis and travel the ninety mile trip together each week.

While there, I had to act the part of a healthy and sober Christian man. I was going through so much at that time in my life. There were times when I would sit in the car or classrooms with nausea, chills, or feeling as though I needed to rush to the bathroom.

My college education allowed me to become a substitute teacher for local schools. Since I had earned the required amount of hours in a four year college and I had no trouble passing a fingerprint and background test, I was deemed eligible to do the one thing I always wanted to do. Teaching was one thing I enjoyed and although I taught classes ranging from kindergarten to adult education, my favorite ages were kindergarten through the fifth grade.

Teaching allowed me the opportunity to stand, sit, walk around the room as needed and feel as though I was giving back to society. I fell in love with teaching and working with children on a somewhat regular basis. Since I was receiving Social Security Disability benefits, I had to report my wages on a regular basis and could only work so many hours, which worked out well for me and my physical condition.

Even while I was teaching, I was using on a regular basis. I would work taking medications around my schedule and attempt to use lighter in the morning, then pour them on heavy once I was home in the afternoon. I used during the days I was teaching and I covered it well manipulating my circumstances. If there was any question, the injury I had sustained and the pain I lived with, was a good excuse to cover any action or weird behavior others may have noticed. I loved the kids and the kids loved me.

Also, during this time period, I was employed part time at a local dry cleaning business. This allowed me the opportunity to work alone, use as I needed and I was able to do my job without any questions, mistakes or complaints. The owner of this establishment knew about my injury, surgeries, attending college, working as substitute teacher and was supportive.

Using was the main reason for my existence, but I wanted so much to be a success, a person my wife, God, children, parents and those who loved me could be proud of. I was a college graduate, substitute teacher, part-time clerk, father, friend, elder at church and full blown addict. What a mess—trying to be one person and living as another. I was the master of manipulation, but one thing I could not manipulate was the level of depression and anxiety this flawed lifestyle provided. I continued to experience high levels of depression and anxiety, enough to keep me living with continual suicidal thoughts, through both my failures and successes.

To My Rescue

Throughout this time, I had some people in my life who attempted to pull me out of my self-defeating and deadly cycle. People who saw the pain, misery, sadness and black hole I was in and reached out their hand to assist me. One of these amazing people was Dr. Thomas Kaye from my hometown.

I first met Dr. Kaye in the late nineties when I became a patient at his practice. When I first went to Dr. Kaye, I had already had a few back surgeries, an internal pump and was addicted to prescription pain medication. I went to see him for high blood pressure, depression and anxiety issues and from then on, he did everything in his power to help me in any way possible.

When I first met him, he was in his mid-forties and full of energy and pep when he walked into the examination room. He brought with him a breath of fresh air, a large amount of positive energy and comic relief.

I could go in to see Dr. Kaye feeling depressed, down and defeated and come out with a sense of relief, new insight and hope. Over the past several years, this man saw me at my worst and my best. He saw me struggling with depression, suicidal thoughts, anxiety, physical illness and addiction and never once did he blow me off as a lost cause.

I was able to open up with Dr. Kaye right from the start about the issues I was dealing with. I shared with him my addiction behaviors, the suicidal thoughts, the cravings for more and more meds, and over time, I laid some of my most personal realities on the line and owned up to what I had never told anyone in the past, even my wife or children.

No matter what I said, did or thought, Dr. Kaye was always there to listen. He even gave me his cell phone number so when I felt as though things were getting out of control, I could call him. In a short period of time, Dr. Kaye became more than a doctor to me; he became a friend who told it as it was, even if I didn't want to hear what he had to say. He always stated what he thought and gave me intelligent and caring options for problems both easy and difficult to deal with.

After getting to know me better and what I was dealing with, Dr. Kaye even reached out and agreed to go to an AA meeting with me. He offered to take me several times, but each time I refused, not willing to even think of giving up my beloved drugs or addiction. But as time went on and Dr. Kaye continued to offer, I finally gave in and agreed to meet him one Saturday morning to attend a meeting.

I thought the only way I could attend a meeting was if I was buzzed, so before meeting him, I loaded up on meds. His idea was recovery for me and my idea was just to make him happy and not lose his support or friendship. Of course, addiction had warped my thinking and made me believe Dr. Kaye would drop me if I didn't do as he wanted. I attended the meeting and as soon as it was over, I was out of the building, back in my car and down the road.

After the meeting, he continued to ask me again and again, even though I continued to give him one excuse after another. All he wanted for me was a better way of life and he was willing to go the extra mile to help me find it. Sadly, I was not willing or ready to take his offer or the initiative to take the first step toward recovery.

I was blessed to find a physician who took the time to think about me, the patient, while I was in his care. What I respected about Dr. Kaye was he took the time to get to know me, to research my health history, and he looked at my chart before entering the room. I know from firsthand experience, this kind of doctor was hard to find.

Dr. Kaye had my back the entire time and was willing and able to get me in recovery, much earlier than I decided to participate. However, it took time, negative consequences, prayer, open mindedness, willingness and honesty to get me in recovery. Each time Dr. Kaye reached out to me, he presented me with another piece of the puzzle, not knowing each and every piece was going to be just as important as the final piece. Realizing my life was out of control, I needed to humble myself and realize recovery was the better choice.

My wife called Dr. Kaye late one afternoon after his office had already closed and he told her to bring me to his office as soon as she could. When we arrived at his closed office, only his car was in the parking lot and when we walked in he greeted us and brought us back to an examination room. He asked if I had had enough yet, and I looked back at him and nodded yes, I had.

He felt I needed the best and wanted me to get in the car first thing in the morning and travel to the Mayo Clinic in Rochester, MN. He would write up a referral and send it with me in hope of allowing me to get in quicker. Before sending me away, he looked at me and stated it was time for me to take this serious. He said I had been through enough, didn't need to go through this anymore and recovery was an answer I just needed to grab.

I had taken enough pills during the day to kill an elephant and that night I was physically, mentally, emotionally and spiritually exhausted. I was ready to throw in the towel. I was so tired of acting as if everything was okay, faking my way through life and being ill from the side effects of the drugs. I was tired of lying, cheating and stealing. Tired of manipulating and sick and tired of being sick and tired. With that, I agreed to take Dr. Kaye's advice and do as he asked. He hugged me, then and there, and I needed that hug more than anything.

Laying it On the Line

My drive from Muskegon, MI to Rochester, MN was an eleven hour drive where I felt fear, sadness, failure, anxiety and shame. But I did have a glimmer of hope.

My wife was not able to make the trip with me due to work and home responsibilities, but my sixty-six year old mother was with me.

When we arrived in Minnesota, we had no idea where we were going to stay or even where the registration office for the Mayo Clinic Services was located. We found a hotel located near Mayo Clinic and while registering, we asked how far we were from the admissions department of the clinic. The clerk filled us in on exactly where to go and even gave us a map of the Mayo Clinic Campus. She shared that with no appointment, we needed to arrive at the appropriate building when they opened. She told us on some days the admissions office was extremely busy and it could be an all day wait just to speak with a Mayo Clinic Representative.

We turned in early knowing the next day meant an early morning and probably a long day. Throughout this trip, I had been taking my own self prescribed doses of medications to keep me comfortable, but even being high did not stop me from being scared to death about what was going to happen the next day.

What was I doing here? Did I really think they were going to help me? Were they going to take away my meds? I had so many questions it felt like my head was going to spin off like a toy top.

Although I had these questions, I knew if I didn't do something, I was going to die. Lying in bed, I wondered if dying would be that bad. Maybe it was the best answer for me at this time, to put me out of my misery and allow my family to move on with their lives, without me holding them down. My death would end the lying, cheating, stealing and manipulating. It would also end the pain.

Addiction had me believing, without a doubt, the world would be a much better place without me. Addiction had me so brainwashed, I couldn't even fathom the possibility of recovery, nor could I see a life worth living.

After lying there having these negative and catastrophizing thoughts for hours, I did what any good addict would do: I got up and took more pills. My cure for everything was more meds. I didn't even care what I took, as long as I had more in my system. Looking back, God had a plan for me, a plan I could not see or even imagine, but it was there none-the-less. Otherwise, I can't imagine how I continued to breathe with so many meds in my blood stream.

The next morning, my mother and I got up and dressed. Like any other morning, I felt like crap due to the countless meds I had mixed, overused and swallowed the night before, but just like any other day, the show had to go on and I had to continue to move forward in some manner.

After a quick breakfast, we began our two block journey to the admissions department at the Mayo Clinic. Once there, we walked in to the large beautiful building, went up a few steps and were amazed at how many other individuals were already waiting.

As I looked around the room, I was overwhelmed by the size of the space, the crowd, the line and just the thought of even being there. What was I going to do? What was I expected to do and what would happen? So I left my mother in line and found the nearest restroom where I did what I did best, used. After swallowing pills, I leaned over the sink and stared into the mirror, looking at an addict in despair, a man totally lost in pain. I was looking at a man who would have to make some decisions, but was unaware of what those decisions would be.

Taking a few minutes to compose myself, I walked back to my mom, who had moved up a few spots in line. I looked around and saw many people with injuries. Some were in wheelchairs, others used walkers, while many others looked healthy and one would never know they were dealing with health issues.

After waiting in line for some time, I was called to a window and greeted by a woman, sitting on a high bar stool type of chair adjacent to a computer. After greeting my mother and I, she asked what she could assist me with. My mother handed her the letter Dr. Kaye had prepared for me and I began to tell the representative why I was there. After I explained my situation, the representative shared they were not taking patients for same day care and she could possibly set me up with an appointment to see one of their physicians, but it might be four to eight weeks before I saw someone face-to-face.

Disappointment must have shown on my face because my mother turned to the representative and asked if there was anything we could do, like stay in town and wait it out. However, the representative made it clear, staying would not increase my chances. Due to the large numbers of new patients, I would have to wait for a scheduled appointment and come back.

"I won't make it to the scheduled appointment," I said.

The representative stopped typing and asked me to repeat what I had just said. "I won't make it to the scheduled appointment."

The Mayo representative asked me what I meant by my statement.

"I will be dead by then. I am living by a thread. "

She asked me how serious I was about what I had said and added it was important for me to be completely honest. I told her I had no doubt if I went home with no help or plan, it would be a deadly mistake.

She got down from her stool, explained she needed to speak with another Mayo staff member and would be right back. My mother stood with tears in her eyes and I was numb, thinking I had come all the way from Michigan and struck out.

Could this really be taking place? Had I wasted time, effort and resources to get here? I was in so much pain and so tired, I started thinking about how I could end it right there in Rochester. However, my mom was with me and I could see she was heartbroken. My parents had never dealt with anything like my addiction and neither of them knew what to say or do. There was nothing they could do to help me, other than just be there, not tip toe around me, not believe my bull crap lines, not accept my self-defeat, and always encourage me toward bigger and better things. When it came down to the bottom line, this was MY fight to fight and MY fight to win or lose.

Just looking at my mom right then should have been enough for me to snap out of my desperate situation. My mom, tears running down both of her cheeks, searching through her purse attempting to find a tissue to wipe those tears away, pulling out one small pink tissue which was not large enough to do the job. The entire time she was looking for the tissue, she just kept repeating, "Your dad and I just don't know what to do for you. We both love you so much and yet we can't do anything to pull you out of this mess."

It must be hell for loved ones to watch addicts fall further and further from them, into the grip of addiction. Loved ones stand by, watch and witness as those they love and care for, fall away one piece at a time. By the time addiction take its toll, the person the addict once was, is no longer recognizable. What a helpless feeling to watch as someone you love, chooses to walk away, one step at a time.

It was apparent in my mother's eyes that she realized her son was in serious trouble and needed help. My mother wiped her tears away a few times and by then, the small, pink tissue was beginning to fall into pieces.

Just then, the representative returned and shared that if I would take a seat, another Mayo Clinic representative would be speaking with me soon. She told me this interview would take place in a private room, where the representative could get a better feel of what I was dealing with. My mother told the representative how much she appreciated her assistance and we would be happy to wait to hear my name called. Before walking away, the representative wished me luck and pointed me in the direction of where I should sit so I could hear my name when it was called.

My mom and I found two seats together, which was a miracle due to there being so many other people in this area. We sat there quiet, waiting to hear my name. Neither of us was in a mood to pick up a magazine, as this was not a checkup for a sore throat. This next interview would have a great amount of importance riding on it and I could feel it throughout my body. If I could have, I would have left to use again, but I knew they could call my name anytime and I did not want to miss this opportunity for help, even though I did not know what kind of help I would receive.

It was probably ten minutes later, when a middle aged woman called my name. My mother and I followed her into a private conference room down a short hall and we each took a seat. I knew this next conversation was going to be difficult and I was going to have to lay things on the table.

After sharing my story, I began to cry. I fell to pieces and as I spoke about my issues, it was hard for me to accept this was my life. While sharing, I began to take in the severity of my situation. It took me a long time to arrive at this point and I knew it was going to take a near miracle to get me out of this mess. I was crying, more like sobbing, attempting to just get words and thoughts out in between gasps for air. All the while, I was thinking what a loser I probably appeared to be. It's just like an addict to get wrapped up in thoughts while unloading their heart.

Am I Crazy?

After what seemed like eternity speaking with the second Mayo Clinic representative, putting my cards on the table, being completely honest and genuine, my mother and I found ourselves on a shuttle, being transported from the admissions department, to one of the Mayo Clinic emergency rooms.

While on the shuttle, my mom and I were definitely in emotional shock. What a morning, going from feeling as though I was going home one minute, to finding ourselves in a shuttle being transported to an emergency room the next. As we sat there together on one of the small seats in the shuttle, my mother sat staring out the window and then looked at me and said she had no idea where we were.

"It will be okay, they will help us find our way," I said.

As each moment went by and we drove further away from the admissions department, my mother became a bit more nervous about becoming lost. My mother worried they were going to hospitalize me and she would never be able to find the hotel or the car we drove, leaving her homeless and helpless.

The shuttle ride from the admissions building to the emergency room took about fifteen minutes and we were delivered right at the front door of the emergency room at St. Mary's Hospital.

We walked in the two sets of automatic doors and up to the receptionist at the window. After stating my name, the receptionist told us they were waiting on me and we could come through the locked doors to meet her in the emergency room.

About an hour later, after being seen by an emergency room physician and sharing my physical, mental and addiction status, I was told they were looking into possible options that might benefit me and my current situation. My mother and I sat patiently, my mother still absorbed with being lost and how she would get back to the hotel and our car.

I was lying back on an emergency room bed, with red and itchy eyes from what seemed like hours of crying and just wanting to get to the bathroom to use. My usual answer for everything was to use: if I was happy I would use, if I was tired I would use, if I was disappointed I would use, if I was worried I would use.

However, I had not used in three to four hours, making my current situation much worse. I was thinking about sending my mother out of the curtain surrounded room, so I could get up and dig in the pockets of my pants hanging in a small locker to find something to provide me some relief. I was feeling a bit intimidated by the surroundings, which was odd for me, as I knew I had just tattled on myself and the hospital staff could have been watching me.

After about two hours of sitting in the emergency room, the doctor came in and told me they had found a room and I would be admitted as soon as possible. The emergency room physician sat down on the chair next to the bed and stated the room was in the Mayo Clinic's Psychiatric ward, which was located in a building adjacent to St. Mary's Hospital. He went on to say that this department would be best suited to assist me with the issues I came to Mayo with and then they could involve the appropriate doctors, tests, assessments and treatment, which would allow me the best opportunity at success.

As soon as he told me what I could expect and kindly wished me the best of luck, he left my room and my mother fell apart. She began to cry, feeling totally lost, out of her element, and concerned for me and my situation. Together we sat there while I attempted to keep her strong and her not knowing what to feel. Thankfully, it was only maybe twenty minutes and an orderly with a wheel chair came into my room and said he was there to bring me to my room. After glancing at my mother, he asked her if she was okay.

"Yes, I just don't know how I will get back to my hotel and car. I have no idea where I am. "

The orderly told my mother she did not have to worry, as he would make sure plans were made for someone to assist her in getting back to the hotel.

I was now in my room, my mother's car was in the correct hospital parking garage, and she was in a new and better located hotel. We had succeeded in our first step of getting me help in some form, and her feeling safe and at ease.

While admitted in this psychiatric ward, I found it much like the rehabilitation centers I had been in several times at home. I was expected to attend group and one-on-one counseling, psychiatrist appointments, recreational activities and there was the all-important community room for eating, watching TV, visiting with others and getting the feel of what was going on with others and how this ward ticked.

By far, the hardest thing to deal with while being admitted to this ward was the sickness from withdrawal I began to experience. I was accustomed to using when and where I wanted and that came to a quick halt when I was admitted. I now was only allowed to take the doses actually prescribed by the doctors.

To say the least, my body was used to my "prescribed" levels, not the doctors'. I was becoming sicker by the minute with diarrhea, upset stomach, chills, headaches, hallucinations and general withdrawal symptoms. Attending the group meetings and counseling sessions was hard, feeling the way I did, but I made it to all of them. I had decided to try this recovery thing by doing what they required of me, with no questions and no reservations.

The first few days in the ward were difficult. Each day I felt worse due to the withdrawal symptoms, which did not shock me since I had been through this before. However, since my addiction had become worse over time and I was using more and more, the withdrawal symptoms seemed worse.

I had tremors, trouble sleeping, eating, drinking, keeping things down, my mouth felt like I had cotton tucked in it and I felt like I was living in a freezer—always cold and having chills. However, I was determined to follow through. I had cried and shared my entire story with the Mayo Clinic Representative in the admissions department and I knew they went through hoops to get me in here, so I had to do whatever it took to succeed.

I got up each morning, showered, dressed, ate with the others, and attended and participated in groups. I was honest when I shared with the psychiatrists what I was dealing with, lined up for meds and took them as requested. I participated in any other activities or groups that were requested of me and never complained.

I also sat in the community room and listened to the others. I was amazed at the issues that had brought some of the others to this facility. There were others dealing with severe depression issues, anxiety, suicidal thoughts and behaviors, bipolar disorder and countless other personality disorders and other mental issues.

What was different about Mayo were the tests. They ranged from brain wave testing, heart testing, sleep testing, several blood tests, personality tests and psychological tests. Never in my past was I put through such thorough testing in order to find out where I stood. Some of these tests were hard; the sleep testing required I remain awake for hours beforehand, so the staff made sure I did not sleep the night before the test. In addition, I found it difficult to participate in some of the other hands-on test because of the withdrawal symptoms, but I did my best and completed each of them.

Needless to say, my only visitor while admitted to the Mayo Clinic psychiatric unit was my mom. She would come to see me every evening during visiting hours and I would attempt to catch her up on what the clinic had done each day and some of the things I was working on in group. Meanwhile, my mother would share her stories about the motel and the interesting folks she had met from across the country, who were there to either get medical services or to support loved ones while they received medical services.

Having my mom with me made this experience much easier to handle. I would receive calls from my wife, kids and others from home, but having my mom there meant the world to me.

Not everyone who was admitted to this unit was as lucky; several of the other patients had nobody there to support them. Julie was in her late thirties, maybe five feet two inches, with short, bleached blond hair, thick make-up, clothes that could have been taken from a medieval theater production and a quiet and sober demeanor.

She had been a patient when I arrived and I had heard her speak a few times in the therapy group we attended each morning. She shared she had been admitted for depression, anxiety and suicidal thoughts. In group, Julie shared what she hoped her future would be like.

She wanted a happy marriage, a husband who would work while she stayed home, and children. In addition, Julie talked about how beautiful her children would be and how smart and successful they would become.

When we were not in group, Julie just sat in the community room and stared at the television set, unless she was spoken to. One evening, after taking our bedtime meds and several of the others had gone to bed, Julie and I had an opportunity to have a conversation while sitting in the community room, watching television.

I began the conversation by asking Julie how long she had lived in Rochester. I then asked where she was from originally; if she was married and a few other questions acquaintances would ask. Julie answered each of my questions. She would stop and think about each of her answers before responding and would focus on the television instead of me while answering. She shared she had never been married, but she had a fiancé at home who had been begging her to marry him for some time. In addition, Julie added she had never had children, but she prayed one day she would be a mother.

Following a short conversation about one another, Julie stated she was sad and did not know if she wanted to live. She added she had always been sad, as a child and as an adult. She stated she had been through several treatment centers with no success and she just felt hopeless. Julie shared that the county hospital in Rochester had sent her to this facility and they were trying a new therapy.

Again, after hearing Julie's story, I realized how fortunate I was to have my mom in Rochester with me, to help combat loneliness and to reassure me I had great family support.

Pain, Pain Go Away

I had been in the psych unit for almost three days and was going through a rough time experiencing withdrawal side effects. Since I had not been truthful about the level of prescription drugs I was taking while being admitted, I was being given very few.

That day, Dr. W. Michael Hooten, a tall, good looking man, wearing a suit, came in to meet with me for an evaluation. He walked into my room, said my name and introduced himself with a genuine handshake and a warm smile. During that first meeting, he spent a long time getting to know me as a patient with a long history of back injuries and surgeries, as well as an individual with severe addiction and depression issues.

What was different about this meeting, as opposed to the multiple meetings I had previously with multiple physicians, was the time he took to listen. Dr. Hooten would ask me a question, and then look at me while I answered. He was sitting in the chair next to my bed with his legs crossed and as I spoke, he responded with a slight nod or a quiet verbal hint showing that he was listening to each word I said. I knew right away, this was a man who cared about my situation and took an interest in me, not as just another patient, but as Ken, an individual.

Dr. Hooten asked questions about me, my family, my injury, the medical treatments I had pursued, and my dependence on prescription drugs. After answering all his questions, Dr. Hooten, in a clear and precise manner, repeated my story to me in a revised and shortened version. I was impressed with the level of information he retained without even taking notes. I was so thankful to have someone listening and understanding that I was hurt both physically and mentally.

Dr. Hooten explained to me that he thought he might have an idea that would help, not only with my physical issues with the chronic back pain, but also with my depression and suicidal thoughts. He shared that he was one of the physicians who worked daily with the Mayo Pain Rehabilitation Clinic, located in the same building. He then went on to explain the three week outpatient clinic and treatment goals. He made it clear this Pain Rehabilitation Clinic would not cure my back problems, but he did give me hope that it would give me the tools to live an enjoyable life, despite my condition.

After meeting with Dr. Hooten, we decided I would register for the Pain Rehabilitation Clinic at Mayo. Since the program was very popular, there would be a short wait to get into the actual clinic. I was scheduled to come back about a month later. However, with the new information, trust and hope he had provided, I felt I had nothing to lose and a doctor who cared about my situation. All of this made the month wait seem worthwhile.

After our first meeting, Dr. Hooten made sure I had an appointment and was feeling better about my situation before I left. What a difference to have a doctor take the initiative to follow through and show concern in this manner.

Attending the three week outpatient clinic was one of the best decisions I made. Dr. Hooten and his amazing staff were able to assist me in moving from living in pain and depression, to living with pain and being both happy and productive. While attending the clinic, I had the opportunity to get to know Dr. Hooten and witness the difference he and his staff made in the lives of the individuals they worked with on a daily basis. While attending the clinic, Dr. Hooten challenged me to move from pain ridden, depression, filled with anxiety, addicted to pain killers and numerous other medications, to changing my attitude, lifestyle, physical condition and overall view on life.

Two of his challenges really stood out in my life change. After starting the Pain Rehabilitation Clinic and undergoing a physical evaluation, Dr. Hooten asked me to begin the process of decreasing the level of the drug Dilaudid which was being released into my system through an internal pump for the chronic back pain. He felt I would have a better chance of a productive, happy and genuine life if I would not only decrease the level of Dilaudid, but stop the pump altogether. He assured me I could do this with his assistance and care.

The idea of giving up a drug I depended on, losing the great high, and possibly increasing my back pain terrified me. However, I knew I had arrived at the clinic as a sick and miserable man who needed to change. With my trust of Mayo Clinic and Dr. Hooten, we began the process of decreasing the level of Dilaudid being administered through the pump. I was not happy, but knew I had to do something different. By the time I left the pain clinic, Dr. Hooten had eliminated the Dilaudid dosage by turning my pump down in increments, until it was only filled with a saline solution.

Dr. Hooten also challenged me to move from receiving government funded disability benefits, to finding a vocation that would match my physical, educational and personal abilities and interests. After discussing my vocational situation, Dr. Hooten scheduled an appointment for me to meet with a vocational expert at Mayo Clinic.

This challenge scared me to death. I was receiving full disability benefits through the Social Security Administration and was covered under Medicare for health insurance. With a wife and family at home, why would I give up a steady income to take a risk with the unknown? My vocation became a large part of my recovery and Dr. Hooten was very inspirational in my decisions.

A Glimmer of Hope

Three weeks after attending an intensive pain rehabilitation program at Mayo Clinic, I was released to travel back home. The day I was released to go home I was sicker than a dog. While at the clinic, I watched as others graduated and left the group smiling, happy, with high spirits and hopes. However, my last day was awful. I was so sick from withdrawal, I just felt like staying in the hotel bed and being left alone, but there was no way I would ever get away with that.

On my graduation day, I left feeling like I had a case of the stomach flu, but knew it was not flu; it was the acute effects of drug withdrawal. Most of the others I had seen come and go through the clinic did not have the addiction issues I had, so coming off their lower doses were not as severe and offered them the luxury of feeling great when they graduated and returned home.

My wife and mother-in-law had traveled from Michigan to Minnesota to pick me up. They arrived with such great excitement, only to find me sick and still vomiting, having stomach issues and a serious head fog. I felt as though I was living in another world. Everything was an effort and my mind felt like it was working at a snail's pace. I had lost my energy, my desire to be with others, my outgoing personality and at times, felt my vision was different. I had the chills and sweats at the same time and a dry mouth.

I thought the withdrawal would last a short time and I would go home happy and full of joy like the others I was witnessing. However, that was not in the cards for me and I had to deal with the effects of what I had put my body through and its effort to get rid of all the drugs.

Before I left, my case nurse in the pain rehab unit sat me down and explained that it was not uncommon for individuals to feel like I was. She stated this drug fog could last several months. My nurse reassured me I would leave feeling low, but living with and using the new tools I had been taught, and with time, I would begin to pull out of this sick and emotional fog and begin to live a life that would lead to the happiness, self-esteem and success I had been searching for.

With that knowledge, my wife and mother-in-law loaded my belongings from my hotel room and packed the minivan. I was given the back seat to lay across with a garbage pail next to me for the periodic vomiting episodes. The ride from Minnesota to Michigan seemed like weeks to me, when in reality it was only two days.

Since I was so sick, we stopped at a hotel in southern Wisconsin where I slept in the hotel bed and my wife and mother-in-law went to a local shopping mall. The next morning, we set off for Michigan and I was never so happy to see my house. We arrived home in the late afternoon and I just sat in my Lazy boy chair and tried to get a sense of my new surroundings.

As promised, the days were long at first and I felt sick for a while. I did begin to feel better within a few weeks, and even though the recovery from withdrawal was not quick, it seemed like I never felt better. I promised myself right then and there, I would never misuse my prescriptions or medicines again. I had learned there was a high price to using and I was paying that price now while going through withdrawal.

After about three months of recovering from the withdrawal and following through each day with the tools the Mayo Clinic's Pain Rehabilitation Center had taught me, I decided to take Dr. Michael Hooten's advice and begin to reach out for the assistance I needed with my vocational rehabilitation and see what kind of job opportunities were out there.

I started with creating my own resume so I was able to see some of my accomplishments and not my failures. Reading it over, I felt I had some strong points and things I could offer an employer if given the chance. After creating the resume, I began to search the local paper and reached out a bit and searched the Internet. It seemed as though every job I was interested in required a certain degree, experience or was located out of my area.

While at the Pain Rehabilitation Center, I had met with a Vocational Rehabilitation Specialist and was given a test that offered some insight into what work I may enjoy doing, and where my strengths and talents would be best used. After taking the test, my three strong vocational positions were: ministry, human resources and teaching. So as I created my resume and began to search for a job, the test results ran through my mind.

I found work substitute teaching and I loved my work, the children, school setting and the opportunity to assist others and watch children learn on a daily basis.

I decided I would look further into this field and what it would take for me to earn my teaching degree. I called the college where I had earned my bachelor's degree in Business and Ministry and inquired about what it would take for me to earn my degree there. A few days later, I received the list of classes I would need, an example schedule I could follow and the cost of the education plan. I knew there was no way my wife and I could afford the price at this time but I remembered the vocational expert sharing with me that each state had its own Vocational Rehabilitation Services for people with disabilities.

I searched the Internet and sure enough, the State of Michigan had services called Michigan Rehabilitation Services and it was only a few miles from my home. The vocational expert had stated they might be able to assist me with education, training, job search, placement and coaching if needed. With the information from the Internet, I placed the first call and made my appointment for a group orientation which would allow me the opportunity to learn what kind of services they provided.

A few days later, I was sitting in a room with several other individuals. The first step was to watch a power point presentation which provided general information and afterwards, we sat down with an individual who screened us for what type of services we were looking for or needed. We then set up appointments with the ones she felt was the best fit.

I was set up for two appointments to get started; one for an empowerment group and another with a Vocational Rehabilitation Counselor. The empowerment group was to assist individuals with the courage, self-esteem and initiative to do the work it takes to successfully look for and find employment.

I was clean of drugs but was continuing to deal with the beast of addiction. Addiction was not letting go of me. I came home from the Mayo Clinic with tools for dealing with chronic pain and a plan to have the internal pump removed, but I was not suited up or prepared for the ongoing fight with addiction. Every day was a new day and every day I wanted to use, but I knew if I started again, I would have to go through withdrawal, probably lose all chances of a job, waste the time and effort I had put into the Mayo Clinic's Pain Rehabilitation Center, and let several individuals down. So every day I fought the fight and was surprisingly successful, given the amount of pain I was living with.

My next step in the vocational rehabilitation program was to meet with a counselor one-on-one and talk about the services I could receive through their agency. I was so nervous before this appointment because I never thought I would have to ask for this type of help. To my surprise and delight the counselor I was matched up with was cheery, outgoing, and comical, but also a serious individual named Patti M.

I met with Patti M in her office and it appeared she was either a busy or messy counselor. She had files all over her office during the first appointment and had to move files off a chair so I could sit down. Patti M made me feel at home and I relaxed within minutes of entering her office. She asked me general questions about my life and got to know me a little bit before moving on to the matter at hand.

After talking about what seemed like everything and laughing about miscellaneous things, we got to the serious business of my vocational future. I shared my story about the accident, recovery, pain rehabilitation, education, past job experience, personal interests and talents. Patti M was taking notes but mostly looked as though she was making mental notes of the conversation.

She then asked me what I wanted to do and what my plan was. I shared with her I had my bachelors degree in business and ministry, but the vocational area seemed too diverse and I had decided with my past experience, interests and passion, I wanted to return to college and earn my degree in elementary education and hopefully become a second or third grade teacher.

My main question for Patti M was, "What is the possibility I can get assistance with earning my degree, since my wife and I can't afford for me to return to college on our own?"

Patti M informed me that their services would not assist me in earning another degree. I would have to use the education I had, in order to move forward with their assistance. My heart sank because I did not see any other opportunities. To me, it was clear cut: I would go back to school, earn my degree and become a teacher.

Patti M asked me why I limited myself to that choice. The question took me off my feet as I thought what other choices were there? Patti M shared she had only known me for an hour, but could see several other opportunities which would allow me to become financially independent and use the education I had already earned.

As a matter of fact, Patti M said she had an idea. She swung her chair around, picked up the phone and began speaking with another individual about an internal position they had and if the position was still open. After saying good-bye a few moments later, Patti M hung up the phone and turned her chair back to face me and said she might have a possible opportunity for me.

Before leaving, Patti M and I spoke about other job opportunities, and the importance of a great resume. She also impressed upon me the importance of showing up on time and appropriately dressed for appointments with her, the groups they scheduled for me, and future job interviews. We also made plans to meet again in one week, but Patti M told me as soon as she heard about the internal position, she would give me a call and we might have to meet earlier than the scheduled appointment.

I left her office feeling as though I had just met a new friend. Patti M made me feel anything was possible if I wanted to put the work and effort into it. She would prove to be a big part of my future as well.

Was This a Mistake?

During my three week pain rehabilitation at Mayo, Dr. Hooten had suggested I have my internal pump turned down in increments and shut off. I agreed to follow through with this plan with Dr. Hooten's assistance and when I traveled home to Michigan, I no longer had one of my favorite drugs, Dilaudid, in my pump. I now had a saline and water solution with no medication in it.

Having the pump shut off and the Dilaudid discontinued played a large role in my withdrawal symptoms, as well as making me feel as though I had lost an old friend who I loved. However, it was only one of the drugs I was receiving on a regular basis. With or without the loss of Dilaudid, the symptoms of withdrawal would have been and were terrible. However, I did follow through with the plan and went home with no internal supply of opiates.

Having Dr. Hooten turn down and shut off the pump was one of the hardest decisions I had to make. I had worked hard and nonstop to get the pump, get it refilled, have it turned up on a regular basis and now the decision to turn it off was mind boggling, to say the least. However, I knew I could not go on the way I was and have a life of happiness or success.

This decision still haunts me today. Yep, still today at times, realizing I had the perfect situation and gave it up. By perfect situation, I mean I was receiving a good dose of opiates and no one questioned it, or in reality knew it. Sometimes, when addiction gets a hold of my mind and I give it a tiny amount of power, it will make me feel regret about the decision and have me feeling like a failure. Over time, I have been more successful in dealing with these negative and tempting thoughts and learned how to deal with them when they return to the surface.

Before leaving the Mayo Clinic, Dr. Hooten and I sat down and made a game plan concerning the internal pump. Part of the plan was for me to go home and contact the surgeon in Orlando, Florida who placed the pump in my abdomen to have it removed. Dr. Hooten did not require me to rush home and do this right away, he allowed me some time to feel better before planning this next surgical procedure, but he did want me to follow up with him and let him know when I planned on doing this, so he knew I had followed through with our game plan.

After being home for about three months and feeling somewhat better, I made the difficult call for an appointment with the surgeon to have the pump removed. Two days later, I received a call from the surgeon's office and was told I had an appointment and a surgery date two days after the appointment.

The appointment was scheduled to be in Florida the week before Thanksgiving and I was pretty much a mess about the whole thing. I wanted to have it removed, I trusted Dr. Hooten and I wanted a better life, but I did not want to take the step to officially cut my ties with Dilaudid. My addiction had me so sick at this time and I thought I might need that drug in the future. I was not using anything and had been clean for four months. Things were going okay, but I could still hear my addiction yelling out "What are you doing?"

As I made the travel plans to Florida, I considered canceling several times. I was sick with anxiety about this decision. Was I doing the right thing? Was I doing it too fast? What if I needed it later? It came down to believing in the Pain Rehabilitation Center, the idea more drugs were not better, and there were better ways of dealing with chronic pain such as breathing in the correct manner, bio feedback, exercise, distraction, moderation, meditation, time control and delegation, nutrition, and mostly it came down to trust. Trust in Mayo Clinic, trust in Dr. Hooten and trust in myself.

I did go through with the surgery in Florida, with my mother once again at my side. For days afterwards, I felt as though I had made a big mistake. Once again I questioned what I had done. Now it was irreversible; there was no going back. This was probably one of the best decisions I had made in recent years and I was feeling entirely blue about the whole thing.

Three days after the surgery, I was on my way home and feeling a bit sick. I still felt a low level of the sickness related to withdrawal, but now I was experiencing headaches as well. Traveling home on the plane was a bit uncomfortable with the headache, but I managed to make it home and was glad to be back.

Once I was home, the headaches continued and gradually became worse. They became so bad that two or three days after arriving home, I found myself in the emergency room. My head felt as though it was going to explode, and I couldn't believe I was back in the emergency room again. However, my addiction loved every minute of it. Here I was, right back in the midst of my favorite things, even though I was trying my hardest to stay away.

While in the emergency room, they placed an IV in my arm. Even though I had a headache, I felt a rush knowing something was coming for pain relief and I was in a state of utter joy, knowing my head would be feeling better and I would also get a free high out of it. My addiction now had me loving anything to do with drugs. I loved the sight of needles, not the pain, but the ecstasy from the fluid that ran through the needles. I was like a Pavlovian dog hearing a bell. I saw a needle and knew good things were coming.

Needles were not the only thing in the emergency room that triggered my addiction: the IV bags hanging from the IV rack, the tubes that ran from the IV bag to your arm, these things also brought pleasant and exciting thoughts to my mind and to this day, I still have those feelings. So even though I was suffering from a severe headache and lying there in pain, I was aware of my surroundings and excited by the endless possibilities awaiting me.

After the emergency room doctor came in and examined me, he shared with me and my wife he was going to do a blood test, but everything appeared to be okay. The physician stated my incisions from the surgery performed a few days prior looked good and did not appear to be infected. In addition, he shared I did have clear drainage, but it was expected that soon after surgery.

Next came my favorite part: the physician told us he would order a medication which would give me some relief from the headache, while we waited for the blood test results. With those few words, I knew I was going to feel a buzz once again and the best thing about it was, it was authentic. I did have a severe headache and I was being one hundred percent honest.

Only a few short few minutes after the doctor left the room, a nurse came in with a syringe full of a concoction I was sure would not only relieve the headache, but give me the best feeling in the world, the feeling of being buzzed. As I lay there with my head flat, I watched as the nurse shot the contents of the syringe into the port of the IV bag hanging alongside of me. After the nurse was finished inserting the medication, I knew it would only take minutes for this medication to cover my entire head and body like a warm and comforting blanket that created a great sense of healing, relaxation and comfort.

Later that night, I learned my blood tests came back and cleared me of any infection, so they sent me home with a prescription for pain medications for the headaches. However, the headaches did not end there, they only became worse by the hour and the clear drainage from my back continued and seemed worse.

Two days later, I was back in the emergency room complaining of the severe headache again. By the time I came to the emergency room this time, my head felt as though it was going to shoot right off my shoulders. The pain was so intense, I almost could not stand up and I felt I was going to vomit, which I did a few times. In addition, the clear drainage from my back was now severe enough that it was hard to keep up with. The drainage would go through the gauze bandages and then soak into my shirt and down through my pants.

My headaches had reached a point where the lights had to be turned down in the room. The pain had become so severe I did not want to even speak with the doctors, my wife or my parents, who met us there. It was tough for my parents to watch me go through a rough time and not be able to do anything about it. My dad even had tears in his eyes, a sure sign of his powerlessness over the situation.

As usual with emergency room visits, the first thing they did was have me remove my clothes and put on a hospital gown. Next, they inserted an IV into my hand and began a bag of saline solution. The physician came in and asked me about my headache and began a general examination. My wife shared I had also had surgery a few days earlier to remove an internal pain pump and the clear drainage from the incision had not stopped, but had become worse.

At that time, the physician gave the nurse an order for pain medication for the headache. As the nurse left to retrieve the prescribed pain reliever, the doctor continued to examine me. First, he looked into my eyes, and then had me open my mouth, felt my throat, neck and shoulders. While I was sitting up, he looked at my back and the drainage had now soaked through the gauze bandage and my gown, onto the hospital gurney.

While the physician examined me, he asked questions about my recent surgery, past surgeries, back injury, treatments, reason for the pump and why it was removed it. Just then, the nurse returned with a syringe of what I had not only needed, but wanted; she could not shoot the magical liquid into the IV line fast enough. I laid there just waiting for the medication to do the job, but this time, I decided I would attempt to raise the stakes. Even though the pain had decreased, I played it up and when the nurse asked me minutes later if the medication had helped, I said no, I was still experiencing a high level of pain.

Not long after telling blatant lies to the nurse, the physician came in and asked me about my headache pain. I lied to him and stated it was not much better. Don't get me wrong, I may have had some pain, but nothing like I was playing it up to be. All I thought about was getting more. Here I was, not home from pain rehab even five months and I was right back lying and manipulating again. The sad thing was, I now knew I was going against everything I had learned and I was falling right into old addictive behaviors. Addiction never wants us healthy, it wants us dead.

Soon, the nurse came in with another syringe loaded with the liquid that would alter my vision of reality. I was now to the point where I would actually count the seconds it took for the drugs to give me the wonderful, warm and inviting sensation, once they were delivered into my IV. I could almost feel the liquid travel up my arm and into my shoulder, neck and then into my head. Some took longer than others, but each was welcomed like an old friend.

Even though I had now received pain medication, I could still feel an undying headache. It was sharp and as the drugs wore off, the headache began to ache and pound, as if someone was standing behind me banging kitchen pots and pans together. Never in my life had I known such great pain: my back injury and surgeries had definitely been painful, but this head pain was like nothing I had ever experienced before.

After lying in the emergency room for a few hours and having a few shots to alleviate the pain, the ER doctor was not real sure what to do for me. They hospitalized me, seeing the headache was not improving, even with medications. At this point, the medications only allowed me some time of decreased pain, relaxation and rest. In addition, the medications were allowing the beast of addiction to run rampant with my thoughts, wants and needs. I cannot tell you how sick I was that night, physically sick and in pain, but I knew the pain was well worth the high. Now I had two new problems, the headache and the need for drugs I had gone without for four months.

Finding a Needle in a Haystack

After an uncomfortable night in an uncomfortable hospital bed, I still had the headache. Each time I began to feel the pain return, I would push the red button to alert the nurses' station.

During the night, I received two or three injections, each made tolerating the pain for the next hour or two possible, but the pain would return with a vengeance, creep over my head and make thinking, speaking or opening my eyes cumbersome and almost impossible to do.

In addition, the clear drainage leaking from the incision on my back continued to be an issue. Since being at the hospital, they had placed a blue pad under my back, which was used to absorb the drainage. However, they were keeping a close eye on both the pad and the incision itself. Between being asked to move from one side to another in order to check the drainage, and being awakened to give blood or in need of pain medications, that night was not one of my best memories. The only thing that made it manageable was having my old friends with me once again.

By morning, everyone except my wife had left and she was sitting in my darkened room when my original back surgeon came walking in and asked us what was going on. He explained he had received news I was in the hospital and undergone surgery to have my internal pump removed only days before. After listening to my wife repeat the story of what happened over the past few days, I heard him ask me if I could roll over on one side, so he could see the incision site on my back. He wanted to see where they had gone in and removed the catheter inserted into my spine and fed medications from a pump in my abdomen, which had also been removed. After looking at both incisions on my back and my abdomen, my doctor shared he was going to have x-rays and a CAT scan done as soon as possible.

As promised, only minutes after he left, I was taken from my room to the x-ray department to have a CAT scan and x-rays of my lower back. Luckily, just a few minutes before I was rolled out of my room, I was given an injection of opiates and was mentally in a good place while having these tests done.

Of course, being under the influence of opiates made the time fly and before I knew it, I was back in my room with my wife beside me and it felt as though I never left. Next, the physician returned and shared that the tests did not show where the suspected leak was and he was not sure what the next step would be. However, he did reassure me he would not stop until they found what was causing the unbearable headaches and drainage.

Before he left, he shared that the nurse would be coming in and hooking me up to a morphine pump. It would allow me to have pain relief when needed. However, it would only allow me to hit it every so often and then I would have to wait again until I was due more medication.

After he left, I felt the weight of discouragement hit me like a ton of cinder blocks. Had I not followed through like I was asked, not stopped taking medications, not scheduled and undergone a surgery to have my internal pump removed, I would not be back in the hospital using drugs.

I felt discouraged even in the midst of taking opiates, but as I pushed the button releasing a new dose of morphine into my system, I began to forget about the discouragement and floated away into a place where I was okay, a place where I was safe and comfortable, a place only I occupied where I could forget about the pain.

Over the next two days, I had several doctors come in and examine me and assess my current situation. It seemed every doctor asked me the same questions and my wife filled most of them in with the story.

After having doctors from various backgrounds and specialties assess my situation, my surgeon came in the next morning and explained they were going to do a blood patch on my spine. Although they could not find the suspected leak, it was clear I was experiencing a spinal fluid loss causing the immense headaches and the drainage from the incision site.

My surgeon explained a blood patch would include having blood drawn from my current IV and then inserted into my spine via a spinal tap. In addition, he stated the blood patch may or may not be successful, but after meeting with and speaking to the physicians who had assessed my situation, they were in agreement this would be the best next step.

It was only an hour or so later when an anesthesiologist and another surgeon came in and introduced themselves. After explaining to me what the blood patch was and how it would help me, he also shared the possible side effects of a spinal blood patch and the ever so popular risks of having such a procedure done. The type of side effects included: infection, increased pain, nerve damage, paralysis and death, the regular list of things that would make anyone want to jump right in and get it done. After explaining what he planned on doing and the dangers, he then told me he would meet me in the surgery room within an hour and he would do his best to help me.

What was going on? I gave up my pump and now this: a spinal tap and they couldn't even promise me it was going to work. I needed relief and although the pain meds were helping, they were not covering all the pain I was experiencing. Now I was starting to get brave enough to ask for more morphine and added injections of Demerol.

As promised, an hour later, I was in the surgery room. Even though I was medicated and in a good spot mentally, I was awake and I can still vividly remember the uncomfortable and painful feeling of having the blood taken from my arm and surgically placed into my spine, via a spinal tap, with the hope it would clot and stop the spinal leak.

Afterwards, I found myself in my hospital room lying flat and feeling hopeful they had found and repaired the leak causing the severe headaches and drainage. In addition, my wife, parents, children and friends were feeling a bit relieved they had found the problem and the solution.

After learning the blood patch was not successful, I underwent the same surgery, not one more time, but three. Each of the surgical experiences brought with it the same uncomfortable and painful feeling and the same hopes of a repair. However, each of the spinal blood patches failed and I was still experiencing the awful headaches and spinal drainage.

I had now been a patient in the hospital for about three weeks and with each day, I became more discouraged. Each day brought with it the continuing headache, the spinal drainage and feelings of hopelessness. However, there was one bright spot in this experience—the pain meds. Although I felt discouraged about the headache and back issue, my addiction loved every second of the attention it was receiving.

I would be clear headed one moment and could relate and communicate with those around me and then the next moment, I would be off into my own safe place where my addiction felt the most at home.

In reality, I believe and know the drugs and their effects were more important to me than the doctors finding the true issue causing me the pain. I was more concerned about getting the next high, than I was about finding out what was wrong with me and how we could repair and heal the situation.

After spending three weeks in the hospital and having countless physicians, surgeons and specialists assess my situation, a doctor came up with a possible plan. One morning, my surgeon came into my room with one of his associates. The associate introduced himself and shared he had seen a similar situation during his residency. He went on to explain the common similarities and how they diagnosed the other patient's medical issue. At that moment, all I saw was the sincere concern in both my original back surgeon's eyes and in the associate's eyes and realized this was more serious than I had thought.

Right Back to the Start

Lying flat in the hospital bed where I had spent the last three weeks, I listened to my surgeon's associate explain that during his residency, he had seen a similar situation where they figured the patient had a spinal leak, but were not able to locate it.

In that case, the patient had several of the same symptoms I was experiencing. The young associate went on to tell me they came up with a plan to have the patient undergo a myelogram, a test where they inject dye into the spine at several levels and then x-ray the spine for possible problems.

According to the associate surgeon, they were successful in using these two different tests together in finding the patient's projected spinal leak. Although he was hopeful the procedures would assist in finding my suspected leak, he did share he was not one hundred percent sure it would work and at this point, but was a good next option.

After listening to my surgeon and his associate, I responded by stating, "Let's go for it."

Although I was in agreement with the plan and I felt their concern and care, I was more concerned about pushing the button on my morphine pump. There's nothing better than the warmth and care a dose of morphine supplies and releases over your body.

After the surgeons left my room, I pressed the morphine button and spoke to my wife about the test. My wife was in total agreement with my decision to move forward and prayed they would find the spinal leak. After just a few minutes, I was in my safe place, feeling comfortable and safe.

It was at that time, my wife shared she had received a message from Carolyn, the manager at Michigan Rehabilitation Services. Carolyn said she had received my resume from Patti M, a Vocational Rehabilitation Counselor, and she was interested in setting up an interview for an available position.

Good thing I was under the influence of morphine when I heard the news, otherwise, I would have had an anxiety attack. This call was the next step in the plan with Dr. Hooten when I returned home from the Mayo Clinic's Pain Rehab Center. However, this spinal issue was not in the plan and I had to deal with it first.

Besides, now I was back on drugs and knew in my heart I was in trouble, or should I say, in the grips of addiction once again. Although I knew the drugs were a problem, I was excited they had called about a possible job opportunity. There was nothing I wanted more than a job, responsibility and an opportunity to get off Social Security benefits.

Seeing the concern in my eyes about the timing of this interview, my wife said it would work out. I had heard that several times before, from doctors, family and friends and look where it got me. Even under the influence of morphine, I was feeling stressed out by this opportunity and its timing.

Minutes later, the nurse came in and told my wife and me I was scheduled to have the myelogram and CT scan. My wife called my parents and her parents and by the time they were taking me down for the tests, there was a room full of people there to pray for the success of the tests and to be there to comfort and support my wife.

As I was being rolled out of my room for the tests, my Dad looked at me and said everything would be okay. My wife kissed me and said she loved me and the rest of the large group wished me well and told me they would be praying they would find what they were looking for.

By this time, I had grown fond of my nurses, doctors, housekeepers, and just about anybody I came in contact with. What was interesting was when they wheeled me into the actual testing room, there were some of the hospital employees there to wish me well and say a prayer for me; that was amazing in my book. I would never forget the show of love, kindness and support.

During the painful myelogram test, I followed instructions and held still and breathed when told. Technicians were kind and supportive during the test and chatted with me about my kids and life in general. After the myelogram was completed and the dye was injected, they rolled me into the CAT scan to have the all-important pictures taken of my back, in hopes of locating the possible leak.

Once on the CAT scan table and lying flat with a few pillows under my legs for comfort, the technician shared I had to stay still and breathe when asked. The technician would take a picture, the radiologist would read it and then they would go on to the next level or picture. After about only four or five pictures, the technician came in, took hold of my hand and stated they had found not one leak, but three leaks in my spine.

Early afternoon, both my back surgeon and his associate returned to my room to explain the findings of the test and what the next step would be. With smiles, they both shared they were happy to tell me they were successful in finding three leaks. The associate shared that according to the pictures, every time my heart beat, spinal fluid shot out of my spine. It was obvious both physicians were relieved they had found the leaks. Now, it was time to decide how to repair the leaks.

Once again, the associate stepped in, took the lead and stated he believed the best plan was to go in and patch the leaks surgically. Thankfully, he had done this before with the same patient during his residency. I did not have to think about this option, and gave my approval Of course, there were two huge pay offs for me: one, the relief and healing it would give me and two, another chance to hear the words "count backwards from ten" while being put to sleep for surgery. Like an addict, I was always thinking and dreaming about the next and better high.

The next day, my back surgeon and his associate teamed up to perform the surgery. After about two hours in surgery, they came out and shared with my wife and large support group, they believed the surgery was successful in patching the leaks and time would tell if they were or not.

Once again, I was waking up from another serious back surgery. Although being put to sleep was something I enjoyed, waking up from surgery was another story; an experience I liken to the flu and a story better left untold. However, hearing from the nurse in the recovery room that all went well was a good feeling and a big relief. Now my thoughts went back to when my next dose of morphine would come.

Hours later, I was back in my room surrounded by family and friends who were ecstatic the surgeons had found the source of my pain and drainage. Although I was relieved they had found the leaks and attempted to patch them, I was tired from the entire experience. I felt overwhelmed by the whole situation, and surrounded by my jubilant family and friends, I realized just how sick I truly was.

Up to this point, I had hung in there and counted on my good old friends—drugs—to get me through. Now, knowing the tests, injections, procedures and surgeries were done, along with the symptoms, I felt physically exhausted and mentally whipped. I just wanted everyone to go home and leave me alone with my good old friend morphine. I wanted to be isolated and go to the safe, comforting and familiar place morphine and drugs created for me.

The next day, still in the hospital, I returned the call to Michigan Rehabilitation Services and spoke with Carolyn, the manager. I thanked her for calling me and stated I would be glad to make an appointment for an interview. I knew I was in no shape to attend a job interview and thankfully Carolyn offered me two or three different times for us to meet: one the following day, the second three days away and the final time was five days away. I agreed to the last time slot and told her I was looking forward to meeting her.

I had some recovering to do and had no idea how I would realistically make the interview. However, I was up to the challenge and truly believed with my good old friends, drugs and manipulation; I would make the appointment and nail the interview. Over the next few days I began to feel better as the headaches subsided and the drainage all but stopped. Two days after the surgery, I was up and walking around the room and hospital ward floor.

Now I had a goal and I wanted to make it to the interview and take the next step in my plan of self-sufficiency. However, I knew I had to beat the odds and I also had to let my doctor know I had set this appointment up. First, I told my wife and after talking about it and her knowing I wanted the job more than anything, she agreed to support me. Next, my wife and I spoke to the doctor about my pending interview.

He had been with me since the beginning: the accident itself and the first back surgery, physical therapy and rehabilitation, another surgery and follow up as well. As a matter of fact, this was the orthopedic surgeon who suggested I apply for Social Security Disability Benefits. After pleading my case, my surgeon was quiet, appearing to think about what I had just told him. After what seemed like forever, but was probably only a few seconds, he stated he would work with me and do whatever he could to assist me in making it happen.

I was released the day of the interview and worked it out with my surgeon to return as soon as I had completed the interview. I showered, shaved and dressed for the interview at the hospital with the clothes my wife had brought me. My parents were kind enough to drive me to the interview. I had them drop me off behind the building I was to interview in, so it was not obvious I had not been able to drive myself.

During the interview, I faked it until I made it. I walked in standing up straight and in immense pain. However, it did not show and inside I was determined, focused and excited for this opportunity. I lived with back pain for years before this interview and even though this pain was much more severe and I had just undergone several blood patches and spine surgery, I was familiar with faking it and making it look as though I was healthier and happier than I was. Besides, I had just taken a dose of morphine less than an hour prior to this interview, and was feeling as though I had my good old friend addiction there to encourage, comfort and cheer me on.

After meeting Carolyn, the manager at MRS, and the other MRS employees who were taking part in the interview, we sat down and got started. I remember thinking it was a good thing my wife and I thought about the clothes I would wear. Instead of wearing a suit and tie like I normally would, we decided it would be smarter to wear dress pants, dress shirt and tie with a loose fitting leather coat. My clothing allowed me the movement needed to sit and stand with some normality. As I sat in the chair, I felt pain shoot up my back and I just had to pretend all was okay and be careful not to show I was in pain. I sat on the front edge of the seat instead of sitting way back, leaning forward slightly keeping my back somewhat comfortable.

The interview lasted about forty-five minutes and I shook hands with each employee who took part in the interview and thanked them for their time. I had never been so thankful to have a meeting over. I was soaking wet from perspiring during the interview. Together, the pain and stress caused my body to react in such a manner. In addition, the morphine probably played a role in my increased perspiring.

Since we were only a mile or so from my home, my parents stopped by my house to allow me to use the re-stroom. While in the bathroom I noticed an increased and unusual painful sensation in my lower back. I had become aware of this new feeling of pain during the interview, but now I had the chance to look at my back. As I lifted my shirt and viewed my back in the mirror, I noticed the incision on my back had turned a blackish-brown color and it appeared as though it was going to explode, much like a volcano. Before I left the hospital, the incision was red and sore, but now it looked totally different and not in a good way.

I felt the incision on my back and it exploded. I now had dark fluids, which looked like old blood, running out of me and all over the bathroom counter. Now what? I had stopped home for a second and now I had a new problem. I called my parents into the bathroom to look at my back and we immediately returned to the hospital. There we learned, after an exam and blood test, I had a staph infection on the back incision.

Could things get any worse? Although I had made it through the interview successfully, I now had a new issue my doctors and I had to deal with. The infection caused me to be in the hospital another seven days. The incision now looked like a large gash, due to the pressure the infection caused and the way it blew open. It took several of the staples with it, leaving me with a large open gash on my lower back that would now have to heal from the inside out. Doctors could not sew or staple it back shut due to the infection, and it now would take much longer to heal and would also take more time for me and the rest of my body to heal.

My addiction was in "I told you so" mode and I was listening to every word it was saying. I was frustrated, depressed and down trodden. The only good thing to come out of this situation was I was still hooked to a morphine machine and receiving other great medications orally.

When I was in my addiction's grip and buzzed, I was safe, not in touch with reality and in my comfort zone. However, when I began to come out of the medication haze, I would begin to think about why I ever wanted to have this done. Why did I decide to have the pump removed? What was I thinking? Of course, Dr. Hooten thought it was a good idea, but he did not have to go through everything I did; he just gave me his opinion. Addiction would tell me I would never get better. I would always rely on drugs and their effects to live. Addiction also told me no one else cared about me like I did. Sure, others would tell me about their great ideas on recovery, but how many of them had even had a need for drugs? How could I listen to people's opinions who never went through a similar situation as mine? They didn't know how much I needed the pills, drugs and addiction to live.

My reality was drugs and addiction. When I wasn't high, I wanted to be. When I wasn't high, I was right back to thinking how could I get high, what more could I ask for, what other problem could I create to get me more. Damn, I was right back where I started: in recovery from a back surgery, infection, intense pain, in a hospital bed, broken down and consumed by addiction.

It's All About the Timing

After recovering in the hospital for three days, I received a call from Carolyn, the manager at MRS. Carolyn greeted me with a warm hello and we went through the usual pleasantries and then she got right to the point. She stated they were quite impressed with me and wanted to offer me the position.

My heart stopped and a myriad of thoughts ran through my mind: they want me, I got the job, this is great, I am so thankful and, now what? I was in the hospital with an open and infected wound, so there would be no faking this one.

Carolyn shared they would like me to start a week from the following Monday, which only gave me ten days to recover and be in shape for my first full-time position in years.

"Thank you and that will be fine," I said, without thinking about what I was saying.

Now what was I going to do? I finally heard the news I had wanted so bad over the past few years, and now I was sicker than a dog. My back was every color of red and brown imaginable and it looked like I had fallen on a bed of hot charcoal briquettes. It was also wide open and filled with gauze in order for it to heal from the inside out. My headaches were much better, but the back pain was still severe and every time I moved, I was reminded I had undergone back surgery and my spine was very sensitive.

Thankfully, I was still attached—both physically and mentally—to the machine that injected morphine on a regular basis. I knew the exact minute I was allowed to push the little button that released another dose of liquid gold to make everything okay. However, I now found myself in a predicament that drugs wouldn't help. So instead of facing the problem realistically, I just pushed my favorite button and minutes later, I was back in a safe place where I thought I had no problems.

Soon the feeling ended and I was dropped right back into the middle of reality. This time when I came back down, my wife was sitting next to my bed. As I regained my senses, I shared with her that I had accepted the job offer and I had to start a week from Monday, which was now only nine days away. My wife looked as though she was computing how many days that gave me for a full recovery, and after doing so, she looked at me and said she did not think I would be well by then.

I didn't think I would be well by then either, but what was I to say? No?

"You might want to call MRS and let them know about your situation," my wife said.

"Are you crazy?" I said. "If I tell them the truth, I will lose the job altogether."

"If the job is meant to be, then they'll wait for you."

"Are you insane?" My belief was no employer was going to wait for a man like me, who had not worked on a regular basis in the past few years, and had serious health issues.

"MRS is a place that works with individuals with disabilities on a daily basis and if anyone will understand your situation, they will," she said.

"I don't care what they do or who they work with on a daily basis, they won't wait for me and I don't want to lose this opportunity," I said. "It will probably be my only true opportunity to work." My mind was set and I was going to be there in nine days fully recovered, healed and back to my hardworking self.

Once we ended the conversation I was back to focusing on when my next dose of medication was since addiction never shuts its mouth. Addiction repeats the same thing over and over: you will never be anyone or anything and you need me to get you through life.

The next few days I tried to come to terms with the job issue. My new job was to start in only seven days and I was still in a hospital bed fighting staph infection and experiencing a large amount of pain. By then, the news of my job opportunity was pretty much public knowledge and most of those around me were happy, but knew I would not be better and ready to work in only one week.

My family and friends tried to get it through to me that I should call and be completely honest. In my heart, I knew calling them was the right thing to do, but I wanted the job so bad and believed it would be my one and only opportunity to succeed. The next day I was released from the hospital to go home, even though I was still in pretty rough physical shape. Part of my release was that a visiting nurse would come to my home, change the dressing and keep a close eye on the infection.

Six days before my job was to start, I began to feel more and more stress as I saw the days go by and realized starting then was not a realistic goal. Even with the aid of my old friends—drugs—I knew I would not be ready. Five days before I was to start, I called Carolyn and told her my reality. After sharing what I had gone through over the past three to four weeks, I told her I understood if they needed to hire someone else.

Carolyn thanked me for calling and being honest with her. She then asked me how my doctor felt about my working after I recovered. I shared with her that he supported my goal of working, but thought I would be held up maybe four to six additional weeks. Carolyn said the job had been there a few weeks before I interviewed and it would not hurt to wait a few extra weeks. She stated I should relax, take time to heal and call her when I knew I was going to be able to work.

Little did Carolyn know I was sitting on my couch in tears. It was amazing to hear someone say they thought enough of me to wait four to six weeks for me to start.

My wife was happy and responded with, "I told you so." She had always been a positive person with faith that things would be okay. My faith at this time was knowing another dose of meds would allow me to be happy and in a safe place for the next few hours. Now that I was home, I no longer had access to morphine. However, I was prescribed Dilaudid and still had a pretty good stash of other opiates and narcotics.

Therefore, I was able to keep myself pretty happy for the next two or three weeks, before I started running low on the pills. At this time, my family doctor knew I was an addict and my back surgeon only allowed me so many pills. So in order to get more of what I wanted and needed, I would have to begin seeing a psychiatrist or two. I would also have to revert to stealing drugs from others if needed.

Over the next few weeks, I began cutting down the number of pills I was taking per day, as I worried about my new job and my addiction. I was still manipulating doctors and getting whatever I could, plus I was looking through other people's houses in order to build my supply. I just wasn't taking as many. Maybe my addiction had become about getting them and not taking them. Within a few weeks, I had stashed up enough to last me quite a while, but was down to taking medications only as prescribed on the bottle.

I wanted to use more than anything, but I knew I had to be clean to start and keep this job. If I was drug tested, I had to be able to answer for the medications they found in my system. My addiction did not like that I was collecting a large arsenal of pills, but not taking them. Remember, addiction wants us dead and six feet under, so by not taking them, I was failing my addiction.

During the two weeks prior to starting my new job, I used three times—meaning I took more than prescribed, a lot more than prescribed. However, I did limit myself to taking the type of medication I was prescribed, in case I was drug tested. I didn't want to lose this opportunity because of my stupidity.

Like Studying for a Test

My back now looked like a road map with scars of various sizes, shapes and depths located from my waist, to up near my shoulder blades. My abdomen had several scars from the internal pumps. With each of these surgeries came more and more scar tissue and I could now feel lumps, much like hardboiled eggs, on each side of my abdomen where the pumps were once located. Just rubbing my back with my fingers, I could feel the buildup of scar tissue.

What had I done? The back surgery to repair the original damage, caused by the auto accident, was crucial and imperative for me physically, but, several of the surgeries could have been avoided. Don't get me wrong, I wouldn't shift all the blame on the doctors, as my addiction was the driving force behind most of the additional and questionable surgeries.

My addiction had me manipulating and using just about every individual who walked into my life. This was not a rare occurrence; there were countless individuals, just like me, acting in the same manner. Most people thought addicts had a certain look and according to some in society, an addict was an individual who lived in a box, shelter or slum of some sort. Addicts were seen as panhandlers on the corner of a busy intersection who used the money to feed their addiction. Addicts were thought to be dirty, disease ridden, unkempt, lazy and wore rags for clothes.

That is far from the truth. Addicts come in every shape, size, race, educational background, profession and are present in each of our daily lives. Addicts are young teenagers, high school students, young adults, middle aged housewives, professionals and can even be found in the golden years of retirement.

By this point in my life I had pretty much faked out most people. I was seen as a fun, loving man who was suffering from a painful accident. I was a Sunday school teacher, tutor for young students after school, substitute teacher, deacon and elder at my local church. Not once did anyone confront me on my addiction. Not once did anyone outside my immediate family ask what was wrong.

I went from doctor to doctor, psychiatrist to psychiatrist, and surgeon to surgeon to get what I needed in order to keep up with my snow-balling addiction and no one noticed. That was how this illness worked in many cases. It grew, fed and rotted one's life from the inside out. It began in the individual, found an open space in the mind, and made that person feel accepted, comforted, secure, relaxed and in control, when in reality, everything it set up was false. By the time the addict realized they had a problem, they were in a deep black vortex. The darkness was never-ending and the individual kept falling deeper and deeper.

Each time I made an attempt to get out of the grips of addiction, I fell hard. Like addicts before me, I pretty much thought I would die because of the illness or its effects. If it didn't take me from an accidental overdose, it would get me in the end by suicide.

My addiction hated it now that my brain realized that what I was doing was wrong and not just hurting me, but causing pain and chaos in the lives of those I loved and held dear. Knowing this information was not enough to make me stop. Knowing was passive and doing something about it took action, a big step I had not bought into and was not willing to take.

I started my new job and achieved my goal of being healthy and able to do so with the help and assistance from others. I showed up for the job and was surprised to hear the job was a Social Security liaison for a state funded rehabilitation service. My responsibilities included informing others with disabilities about the government funded programs in place to aid clients in finding suitable and attainable full time employment. I obviously hadn't listened very well at my interview and was now faced with a job I knew nothing about.

I began learning the job one step at a time. I had been hired as a manager of sorts and was responsible for the employees who worked under me in MRS satellite offices located in surrounding areas.

During the first few months, I learned the basics about the services MRS provided such as: evaluation, learning assessments, aptitude assessments, education, training, job search and placement and job coaching, in hopes of finding permanent employment for individuals with limiting disabilities. MRS also aided those with physical impairments in purchasing equipment, which would allow them to be successful in finding and keeping long term employment.

As I went through the training phase of this position, I attempted to take just one day at a time. My new position was utilizing the education I had received through my college work and I was grateful I had used my time off to earn my Bachelor's degree in Business.

After about two months, I was beginning to feel somewhat comfortable in my new position. I was blessed to have a district manager, regional manager and training coach who were angels, supporting me from the start.

The most challenging responsibility of this position was learning the information regarding Social Security. Like many individuals, I dreaded receiving government publications because of their underlying details and boring information. My job was to take the information and present it in a manner that people would not only understand, but feel encouraged and excited about working toward a goal of returning to employment.

My job was to inform an individual receiving monthly benefits on a regular and safe basis, that it would be better to have faith and attempt to return to work in a weak economy. For the most part, I loved every minute of it. I was not just preaching it, I was doing it. In learning about the Social Security programs, I learned that I had not just jumped into work without a net. The government had placed safety nets in the system for people with disabilities, like me, attempting to return to work.

I now knew the programs, how they worked and became well versed on the ins and outs of each of their steps. Although this was not an easy sell to those receiving benefits, I knew we were successful in changing some lives.

My position had me traveling a day or two a week, from the main regional office where I worked, to the satellite offices. Together, my team and I were doing a good job getting the information out. I thought when I began this position that I, along with those I worked with, could instruct and inform in such a manner that would excite and promote others to jump right in and try to better their quality of life. However, I was not prepared for balance or realistic goals, high expectations for myself, or reality when it struck.

After returning home from the last hospitalization and recovering from spinal leaks and infection, I attempted to watch my drug intake. After all, I had only weeks to clean up my act, get straight, and be prepared for a possible drug test. I was aware a positive drug test could cost me this job and I wanted to return to the work force. I started this job with confidence, strength and courage, but it did not take long for addiction to attack me once again. Make no mistake, addiction was cunning, baffling, and attacked in any form it could.

Not Again

Working alongside, and in the best interest of others much like me who were disabled and receiving Social Security benefits, was challenging, disappointing, tiring and rewarding at the same time. Every day I met with people who wanted a life which included work, but were too fearful of attempting to follow the government's outlined plan and take advantage of the safety nets placed within the program for them.

I don't know if it was the pressure of my perfectionism and feeling I was not having enough success, the intense back pain, or the anxiety of allowing me to utilize the government's safety net for myself. Whatever it was, it opened enough space in my mind to allow my old friend addiction to walk back in and take hold.

It started slowly by adding a few extra pills to each dose every few hours. Since my addiction started up from where I left off before surgery, I was now taking more pills than I could count in one day—a few here, a handful there and in a short time, I was right back into full blown addiction.

It didn't happen overnight, but it wasn't far off. I had been working for the state for about six months and using prescription drugs as a buffer to live with my reality. I had become dependent on drugs in the past and I knew they were friends I could rely on at a moment's notice. No questions, no nagging, no long conversations, no condemnation or judgment, just pure welcomed relief. I could bring my friends everywhere with me in their little orange bottles in a back-pack, computer bag, lunch bag, or I could leave them in my car. In addition, most people knew about my back issues and that I had gone through quite an ordeal with it, so if they witnessed me taking a pill or two, it was understandable and acceptable.

Seven months after beginning my new job, I found myself hiding a considerable sized addiction to prescription drugs again. I was still functioning well and most people did not know I was struggling, since most of my co-employees did not know me before and would not have noticed a difference.

I was still presenting the information about the government work incentive, called Ticket to Work, and assisting others one-on-one in seeing the advantages of giving it a try, all while I was using drugs on a heavy and regular basis. Here I had worked for this opportunity, wanted it more than anything, was proud to be gainfully employed and now let addiction take the reins again.

Addiction would speak to me and I listened. It spoke on a daily basis almost nonstop when my mind was idle and say things like: Who do you think you are? Do you really think you can do this? Do you think you will be successful? You know you need me more than any job. So much for the courage, strength and excitement I began this great job opportunity armed with. Now I was once again sick, addicted and trapped.

I should have been nominated for an Oscar during this time. Much like other addicts out there functioning on a regular basis and living from day-to-day, minute-to-minute, and at times from second-to-second; I was living a complete lie. I was smiling, laughing and working on the outside and hurting, crying and dying on the inside. However, I wanted this job and I was going to do it and do it one hundred percent, even if it killed me.

Relief with Reluctance

Eight months into my new job, my wife and I were invited to a summer wedding. The weather was beautiful in West Michigan and the wedding was going to be held outside. On the day of the wedding, we stopped at a large retail store to purchase a gift for the newly married couple. As always, when going through the check-out, I purchased an empty self-serve plastic soda cup. I was not only addicted to pills, I was also addicted to Diet Coke©.

While my wife stayed at the checkout counter and purchased the gift, I made my way to the self-serve soda dispenser about thirty feet away. Seconds later, I found myself on my back on the floor, in shock and totally embarrassed. I had walked up to the soda dispenser, stepped on several ice cubes on the floor, and then fallen.

Here I was a six-foot-five man, weighing two hundred and fifty pounds, and I was lying on the floor, flat on my back. At first, due to the embarrassment, I had forgotten about my back and was more worried about how stupid I looked.

"Ken, are you okay?" my wife asked.

"I think so," I said. After lying there for about two to three minutes, a store manager asked if I was okay. I got up from the floor, still a bit shocked and embarrassed. As I stood up, the reality of the situation began to hit me; I had hit my head on the self-service counter and then fallen flat on my back, which was feeling stiff.

Standing there and eventually filling out an accident report with the manager, I realized how stiff and sore I was beginning to feel. After wrapping up the report, we left with both the wedding gift and my pride somewhat intact.

My wife and I attended the wedding and I made it through the ceremony and a good share of the reception. However, as the night progressed, my pain increased and I became stiffer from the fall.

Over the next few weeks, I attempted to keep the fall on the down low and tried not to talk about the pain or show symptoms from it. I returned back to work as scheduled and never missed a day. I never spoke about the fall at work as I was concerned my employer would see me as a liability. It seemed as though trouble, accidents, pain and disaster followed me around day-to-day.

As the days turned into weeks and weeks turned into months, I noticed the stimulator, my only defense against the pain I had other than pharmaceuticals, was not working on a regular basis. I would feel the electrical stimulation at times and then notice it would turn off and on by itself without me using the remote to do so. I knew there was a problem and I wasn't sure what to do about it.

To tell someone would open a new can of worms, as it would require me to talk about the fall and possibly have my employer find out. My employer had never given me a reason to fear being open about such an event. It was me who was fearful of losing my job, knowing it was my dream to have it. I was working and I did not want to disturb or end this dream.

During this time, I continued using my old friends and in greater amounts. I was a walking, talking, complete potential liability in the making. I had multiple pain patches on under my clothes, and I was taking pills by the handful and as often as possible. I was high much of the time; no, ALL the time. However, I put a smile on my face and just dealt with it in my own manner—with drugs.

The pain eventually became significant enough that I knew I had to get some help. I spoke to my wife about the pain and she made an appointment with the one person I trusted, Dr. Kaye. He knew I valued my job and didn't want to put it in jeopardy.

Two days later, I found myself sitting in an exam room at Dr. Kaye's office. He walked in with a big grin on his face, but he wasn't smiling for long though as he shut the door and took a seat on a stool. Dr. Kaye took one look at me and seemed to instantly know I was using, and using a lot.

Dr. Kaye went from happy go lucky to serious and subdued. He shook his head and looked at me.

"How long is it going to take for you to learn that you're misusing the meds and need help," Dr. Kaye asked. He went silent for a few moments, which didn't happen often. He looked at me, at the floor, and then was silent. I knew he could see right through me.

"If I go with you, will you attend an AA meeting?" Dr. Kaye looked up at me. "I'll meet you tomorrow morning."

I started to answer but he stopped me. "Think about it during our appointment and let me know before you leave."

Dr. Kaye looked at my wife with a smile. "Now what brought you here today?"

I gave him the synopsis of the slip and fall and how I was living with a large increase in back pain. I also told him about the trouble I was having with the stimulator.

"Take your shirt off and lie on the exam table," Dr. Kaye said. He did an exam of my head, neck and torso region and asked me to roll over onto my stomach. He then did a full exam of my back, which was sore and stiff. After the examination, Dr. Kaye stated he was going to request x-rays of my spine to make sure I had not reinjured it in any way. Dr. Kaye also said I was going to have to contact the surgeon in Florida to have the stimulator checked and possibly fixed or replaced.

I shared my reservations about having the stimulator checked.

"What is more important? Your health or your job?" Dr. Kaye asked.

It sounded like an easy question to answer, but I truly felt I would never get another job opportunity. Addiction had me believing I would always need the pills and medications and I would never be anything without them. Sadly I believed I would never be anything and this was my only opportunity at success. Addiction told me I better lie, hide and use drugs, and keep this a secret from my employer. I had bought into addiction with all my heart, even though I could see the smart, sensible and sober people, such as Dr. Kaye and others, around me telling me I could make it without drugs. I fell for the voice of addiction telling me something fabricated, foolish, extreme and unrealistic.

"Do you know how bad I wanted this job?" I said to Dr. Kaye. "How do I tell them?"

"Be honest and open," he said.

Yeah, right, I thought.

Dr. Kaye reminded me I was working with people with disabilities for a profession and my employer would understand when I told them I fell and possibly hurt myself or damaged the spinal stimulator.

I stood up to leave with thoughts of actually putting a few of Dr. Kaye's opinions into action. Dr. Kaye had also set me up for x-rays and a CAT scan and refilled a few of my blood pressure medications while I was there.

"So, do we have a date tomorrow morning?" Dr. Kaye asked me as I started to walk out of the small exam room.

"I'll be there," I said.

What Did I Get Myself Into?

After leaving Dr. Kaye's office, I knew we would get to the bottom of the situation, yet I was afraid my employer would not understand. I knew they had been great up to this point with me, but would they understand another injury or illness? I was also anxious about the plans we had made for the next morning.

My addiction was screaming—what the hell are you doing? Any time I made plans to take a step toward recovery, my addiction made its disapproval clear by screaming in my head over and over. I did not want to go. I did not want others questioning me. I was not interested in recovery and I did not want to stop using.

Matter of fact, this anxiety about going to a 12-step meeting with my physician, gave me another reason to use that night. I used not only once, but multiples times and did not sleep.

The next morning I showered, combed by hair, brushed my teeth and took a handful of pills. It was a strong and potent assortment that would aid me in getting through this entire situation. I left the house with clean teeth and clean clothes, headed for a support group designed to help people "get clean."

Dr. Kaye was there as promised, happy and energetic. We took two seats close to the door as there were not a lot of empty seats and the large room seemed almost full. A large circle of people sat in chairs along the four walls of the room and in the middle of the room. Six large long tables were put together, creating a large island. Around this island were countless individuals drinking coffee out of white foam coffee cups.

As I sat there, Dr. Kaye attempted to include me in conversations with those around us. He had the natural ability to make others around him feel welcome, comfortable and included. However, that morning my addiction was pissed and so was I. *What the hell am I doing at a 12-step meeting?* I did not want to be there, I did not want to be sober and I certainly did not want to hear others talk about how great their lives were with their so-called recovery plans.

It didn't matter what I wanted or did not want, I respected Dr. Kaye and figured I could do this one thing for him. It was only for an hour and I had prepared beforehand by loading up on pills and was feeling their effects. I was thankful for the drugs which allowed me to feel absent the whole time I was sitting there.

I did attempt to listen to others, but all I could think about was that they were going around the circle taking turns speaking. What would I say? My mouth was going dry, I began to sweat, and I could not feel my legs.

The attention was now focused on Dr. Kaye and I was next. I had no idea what Dr. Kaye was saying, as all I heard was my addiction telling me to get up and walk out. I was lost in a panic. Just as I was about to get up and walk out, I heard Dr. Kaye say thank you for listening and I knew the focus had now shifted to me. I stated my name and said I was an addict. I then stated I just wanted to listen.

"Thank you Ken," I heard everyone say.

After the meeting ended I could not leave fast enough. Once in my car, I took deep breaths. I was completely overwhelmed by Dr. Kaye, the people and the meeting. I did not want to give up my drugs and my addiction was making it clear I couldn't, even if I wanted to. I took an orange bottle out of my car console and took another potent handful of pills to get me through my anxiety.

I drove home in a daze and thought about how stupid I probably sounded to the others and what an idiot I made of myself. I couldn't even remember if I said my name correctly. *I will never do that again,* I thought.

I had survived the ordeal of attending a 12-step meeting, but now I had to face the other ordeal of telling my employer about my slip and fall, the potential damage to my spinal stimulator and the pain I was now living with on a constant basis. Back in active addiction, I knew I would have to rely on drugs to get me though the experience.

At work, I asked the manager if I could speak with her privately. I had loaded up on drugs before coming to work and as I sat at my desk for a few minutes, I took a few more just to settle myself. I truly believed after I told my manager about my situation, she was going to tell me to gather my belongings and hit the road.

I thought about Dr. Kaye and how he was the one who set me up for this disaster. What was he thinking? What was I thinking taking his advice? My addiction's voice was loud and clear: you are a loser. You can't make it without me. After you get fired, I will be here for you.

This was running through my mind as I sat in my boss's office, watching her fish swim around in their large tank.

“What was it you needed to talk to me about?”

Here goes everything, I thought.

After sharing with my boss what had happened, she leaned forward.

"Damn kid, you have bad luck," she said. She asked me more about the slip and fall and somehow my footwear came up. I told her I had been wearing flip-flops and she comically replied I got what I asked for.

“What do you need from us?” she asked.

“I'll need a few days off to fly down to my surgeon in Florida to have the spinal stimulator checked,” I said. “And I'll also need a few days, if not weeks, to have the stimulator surgically repaired.”

By the time our meeting concluded, my boss made it clear I would not lose my job and they would support me any way they could. She also made it clear I needed to take care of myself so I could return to work healthy and ready to take on the job I was hired to do. She said she had been impressed with my job performance and had no doubt I would become successful in anything I set my mind on doing.

Sitting at my desk minutes after meeting with my boss, I was thinking, *did that just happen?* I took a few deep breaths to calm down and accept my reality.

My next step was to contact the surgeon in Florida to have my spinal stimulator checked. I made the call and scheduled an appointment for the next week, knowing I would still have a job when I returned.

Through this entire time, I was using drugs for every high, low and anything in between. Even with Dr. Kaye and my boss supporting me, my addiction was running the show.

Before I left for Florida, I had the CAT scan and x-rays Dr. Kaye had ordered. In addition, I worked right up to the day I was to leave for my scheduled doctor's visit.

Packed, ready and with the CT scan and x-ray results in hand, my mother and I boarded a flight for Florida for another visit with our good friends in Orlando. My parents had met our friend Carolyn at the Mayo Clinic some twenty years earlier. Carolyn and my dad were there for serious health issues when they met. My parents stayed in contact with Carolyn and her family and we had a close and lasting relationship between our two families.

Carolyn and her husband Angelo lived in a beautiful suburb. When I made my first appointment in Orlando with the pain specialist, Carolyn had hosted me and since then, I had stayed with them almost every time for appointments, pump refills, surgeries and follow-ups. They were there with open arms during each of my health issues and made us feel as though we were part of their family. They were family to me and had seen me at my best and my worst.

After arriving in Florida, I saw my surgeon who reviewed my CT scan and x-ray results. He told me the leads that allowed electrical stimulation to run from the actual stimulator to the exact locations in the spinal cord, had been damaged in the fall and they were no longer connected.

He had no other choice but to go in and repair the stimulator in order to get it working once again. I had come this far to have it checked out and I did not want to go home with a non-working stimulator.

Four days later I was in the surgery room awaiting one of my favorite activities, being put to sleep with strong medications. As soon as I walked into the hospital, my mood went from “so-so” to “excited as hell” about the IV I would receive.

While in the hospital, I was not only lucky enough to experience the wonderful feeling of being put out for surgery, but I also received some great pain relievers my addiction loved and enjoyed. My addiction was smiling from ear to ear each time the nurse came in with a syringe and transported me to my heaven.

Two days after surgery I was released from the hospital and staying at my friend Carolyn's house to rest and recover. We planned to stay for a week following the surgery as I had an appointment scheduled with the surgeon the day before I was scheduled to fly home. The surgery had been successful and I could feel the electrical current which brought some relief from the constant pain.

On the third day after the surgery, I started to feel ill, like I was getting the flu. Within one day, I was so sick I was lying on the bathroom floor.

My solution was to use more drugs, which I did, but it did not help the situation. I was nauseous at first, and then I could not stop vomiting. I started having diarrhea and was hoping I would just die.

My mother called the surgeon's office and they told her I probably had the flu and to treat it accordingly. Carolyn and my mom watched over me, but as time went on, I got sicker.

On the fifth day after surgery, things became worse. I was going from the bedroom to the bathroom just to avoid others so I could suffer alone. I felt like I wanted to die and more than once it crossed my mind to take enough meds to shut my system down for good.

My mother decided it was time to do something. She did not agree with the doctor's office and felt something was wrong. Carolyn and my mother assisted me into the car, placed a bucket between my legs and drove me to the local emergency room.

The car ride to the hospital seemed like forever and I was thankful to see the entrance to the emergency room. As

Carolyn pulled up to drop me off at the door, I was hopeful I would get an IV that would provide my favorite type of additional help.

There were people everywhere waiting for help in the emergency room. The large waiting room and the hallways were full of people sitting in wheelchairs and leaning against the walls. People were also waiting in line to check in and my mother stood at the back of the line to check me in.

What a Mess!

I had been in the hospital waiting area for at least a couple of hours and as I listened to the nurse call several other names, I watched other patients either walk back or be transported into the treatment area. I had used in the car on the way so I was feeling okay at this point, but I knew this feeling would not last forever.

After four hours, I asked my mother to ask how much longer we would be waiting. I knew she would have to walk across the large emergency room to the reception desk, which was staffed by three busy women with incoming patients. With my mother away from me, I could take some of the opiates and narcotics mixture in my pocket.

My mother did as I asked and walked to the reception desk. While she was gone, I maneuvered myself in the chair so I could get my hand in my pocket to get the pills and took the handful of pills in two doses. Without something to drink, it made it a bit harder to swallow the pills, but I had never let that stop me before and it would not stop me now.

I was waiting to see a doctor and still swallowing my own prescribed levels of whatever I could. After swallowing the pills, I sat there about twenty minutes before my mother returned stating they could not tell her how much longer it would be.

Fortunately, it wasn't much longer when my name was called. I don't know if it was my mother getting upset or if it was truly my turn, but I was grateful. By the time I was rolled into the emergency exam room, I was feeling the effects of the drugs and was in a pretty good spot mentally, but physically I was very ill.

A nurse came in, took my vitals and asked what brought me to the emergency room. Between my mother and me, we gave her a quick version of my story. After listening to my symptoms and looking at my incision, the nurse stated the doctor would be with me soon. I was then seen by the attending physician and admitted as a patient. However, over the next day and a half, I never received a diagnosis or a remedy, but they kept me happy and comfortable with medications.

I was still lying in a hospital bed three hours before I was scheduled to fly back home to Michigan with diarrhea and vomiting. I had to make the decision to leave the hospital and get home on my previously purchased tickets, or stay where I was not getting anywhere or improving.

After speaking with my wife over the phone several times and talking about my options with my mother, we decided to take a chance and just get me back home. Shortly, I was dressed, unhooked from the morphine drip and in a car on my way to the airport.

The flight home was a three hour panic attack for me. There's nothing worse than being sick on an airplane, surrounded by others who don't want to see you puke or worse, lose control of your bowels. I was trying to stay focused on my breathing and remain in the present, knowing I would be home soon.

The flight crew knew I was ill and made sure I was able to get out of the plane as soon as they opened the door. They also had a wheelchair waiting for me at the gate. My mother pushed me through the airport and when she rolled into the luggage claim area, my father and brother-in-law were standing waiting for us.

We were soon on the road heading for my hometown forty miles west of Grand Rapids. I was so relieved to see my house and get into my own bed. Before going to sleep, I took another concoction of pills and made sure to add a few of the kind I knew helped me sleep. With the amount of pills I took, I am surprised I woke up.

The next morning my wife called Dr. Kaye and told him about my nightmare experience and how ill I was. Although it was a weekend, he told my wife to bring me into the office and he would meet us there. Just as he said, Dr. Kaye was at his office waiting. He examined my back and was a bit concerned about the redness around some of the staples. He cleaned the area around the incision and stated he wanted me back in his office first thing Monday morning.

On Monday morning my wife, insurance RN case worker Patti W, and I were at Dr. Kaye's office. He was going to change the dressing from my surgery and check on the redness. Dr. Kaye had not even taken off the dressing when he stated he did not like what he saw and thought I was in a bit of trouble. He thought the redness appeared worse and looked as though I might have a case of MRSA.

He cleaned and changed the dressing, but less than an hour later he had me in another doctor's office across town waiting to be seen by a surgeon. The surgeon took a blood test and said in his opinion, I did have MRSA and it was gaining strength.

He called my original orthopedic surgeon, who was out of town, but had me in to see one of his associates less than an hour later. When the associate took a look at my back, he told me I was to go to the emergency room and he would meet me there. I was in the hospital by mid-afternoon and had surgery early the same evening.

I had contracted MRSA, a deadly blood infection, and the orthopedic surgeon decided the stimulator had to come out. But I did get anesthesia again and another great morphine pump I used as much as I could. I also received several other medications I counted as old friends and a few new friends who would soon become my best friends.

Little Did I Know

Before and after surgery I was put in isolation, kept separate from the other patients and given a private room so the infection would not spread to others. My doctors, nurses and any other specialists were required to wear protective garments over their clothing, gloves and a mask before entering my room.

I spent close to three weeks in the hospital. I had now lost the spinal stimulator and had plenty of time to think about the reality of living in constant back pain. I became more anxious about getting out and back to taking my own level of drugs. While hospitalized, I received morphine and other pain medications. I was also receiving medications on a regular basis for the blood infection. However, I was definitely feeling the need for more and missed being able to take as much as I wanted when I wanted.

I now had a new doctor on my case, a communicable disease specialist. Dr. Olsen was a middle aged man with a quiet and caring personality. He saw me each day to make sure the incision was healing without further infection and he always took time to talk to me for a few minutes.

Right after surgery, they began treating me with the antibiotic, Vancomycin, to fight the MRSA blood infection. Every day, they would hook up this medication to my IV and let it drip until it had been released. After about a week, Dr. Olsen decided a port should be surgically placed in my arm so when I was released from the hospital, I would be able to receive the IV drip of Vancomycin on a regular basis.

I was rolled down to the surgical room to have the port placed in my arm. By now, you know I was excited to be put out again, but I was disappointed to find out they only give a sedative medication for this procedure. However, a sedative was better than nothing, so I felt the effects of the sedative as it was released in my IV and before I knew it, the new port was placed in my right arm.

The medical staff began using this port for all my medications, but I felt I was not getting enough. So, I began to play the manipulation card and asked each of the doctors and specialists for more pain medication. I knew which doctors I stood a chance with and which doctors never to bring it up to. I manipulated a few to add some pain medication, but nothing worth bragging about. I would manipulate medical professionals and feel as though it was something worth bragging about. How ridiculous was that? Just thinking about it now makes me feel foolish. Even if I could brag about it, who would I brag about it to? Nobody I knew thought like me, so if I were to bring it up with anybody, they would have thought I was insane.

About a week after having the port placed in my arm, Dr. Olsen noticed it did not look right. The port site was now infected by MRSA and it would have to be removed. The doctors were concerned the infection showed up as I was receiving treatments for it every day and it continued to show signs of gaining strength.

Back to the surgical room to have the port removed and a new port placed in the other arm. I was tired and weary from the entire experience. I had dealt with depression on a regular basis before this happened, and now I was beginning to fight an intense battle with depression. Even though I had a constant stream of upbeat visitors, get well greetings, prayers, cards, notes and flowers, my mood was spiraling and I was falling apart piece by piece.

Depression was another old friend I knew well and I was heading down a road not in agreement with the goals I had set while at the Mayo Clinic. I hadn't imagined or pictured running into so many snags and setbacks and I was losing my energy and hope with each new day. Regret, sadness and defeat were surrounding me and I ran faster and faster toward addiction and depression.

Living Two Separate Lives

Now that the port had been surgically moved, I was back in my room surrounded by family and friends. People came and left on a non-stop basis, but I valued and looked forward to my time alone. By time alone, I meant time with addiction and depression, my two friends.

I would focus on what drugs I had taken, what drugs I was being given, and what drugs I could manipulate the medical professionals into prescribing for me. Much of my time was spent thinking about, wishing for and dreaming of drugs.

A few days after the surgery, I was released from the hospital on Christmas Day.

After the holidays, life at home became a regular routine of nurse visits, incision cleaning and packing, IV medication treatments and of course, the all-important oral medications. Within a couple of days of being home, a nurse came and trained me on how to safely give myself the IV medication Vancomycin, and she trained my daughter on how to clean, pack and bandage the incision site. After five days, the nurse only came once a week to check on me.

My first visit back to see Dr. Olsen was six or seven days after my release. As soon as he examined both the incision site and IV port, he became concerned about the infection gaining strength and said I needed to have the port moved again. On the same day, I was again admitted as an outpatient to the hospital and had the port moved from its existing location, to another spot on my arm. Why was the infection still growing and infecting me in new places? This question hounded my team of physicians and the infection was wearing me out.

I was tired of being sick, tired of the surgeries, tired of the infection running through my veins, tired of being sore, tired of seeing medical professionals, tired of not being an active member of society and tired of living. My depression had kicked into high gear, but I was putting on a good face and people thought I was full of strength and hope.

During the next few months, things did not get any better as I had to have the port surgically moved a few more times. Dr. Olsen had become a main stay in my life and I was seeing him on a regular basis. With the medications he prescribed, we continued the fight against MRSA, but the infection continued to fight back and seemed to be outsmarting everyone.

While fighting the infection, I was taking so many pills I could not even keep count. I was taking everything I could get my hands on, my meds, new prescriptions, old prescriptions, other peoples meds, over the counter meds and anything I could use to get high.

As time went on, the addiction took over more and more and it was becoming harder for me to satisfy its consistent and growing hunger. Feeding the addiction took me to parts of town known for trouble that could place an individual in the back seat of a patrol cruiser, in jail, prison or worse yet, the morgue.

Since my addiction had become so severe and it was impossible for me to find enough drugs, I made the decision to look other places. Some were not in the best part of town, but some were almost in my own backyard. Drugs had me doing things I would have never even imagined doing, meeting people I did not know, getting drugs I did not know where they came from, driving around town looking for certain individuals, and spending countless dollars on something that lasted a short time.

During this time, my oldest son, Aaron, was about to get married. He and his beautiful fiancé Kristyn, had given my wife and me our first grandson a year earlier. Aaron and Kristyn had found out they were going to be parents at the start of Aaron's senior year. I remember the night he told us Kristyn was pregnant and I laughed. I knew it wasn't funny, but being under the influence of drugs had me responding in unconventional, and sometimes inappropriate, ways.

About three weeks after Aaron's high school graduation, Kristyn delivered Jayden Mark, our first grandson. Now, almost a year later our son was getting married. I, of course, had to medicate myself to get through the experience. I suited up for the wedding, hid the IV line in the arm of my tux and decided the show must go on. That day, very few people realized how sick I was and I pleased others by showing up and participating. I also pleased myself by taking enough pills to get through the day. God only knows how many pills I took.

My son's wedding and reception were beautiful and went off without a hitch. However, after arriving home late in the evening, I cried because the physical pain was beyond belief. So what did I do? What I always did. I took more medications and went to bed.

With the wedding behind us and the kids on their honeymoon, I was back to my fight with MRSA. Every day it was the same routine of treatments, depression, anxiety, finding drugs, getting drugs, and taking drugs.

A few days after the wedding I was sitting in the living room and could see two large containers of cinnamon schnapps liquor left over from my son's wedding. *If a strong medication takes less than a minute to feel the effects after being administered through the IV line in my arm, how long will it take if I shoot a vial of cinnamon schnapps right into the same IV line?* The thought was all it took for me to start shooting schnapps into my veins. I did not think the first vial hit me fast enough, so as time went on, I decided to shoot more and more. The alcohol did hit my system fast and was a great alternative to the drugs I received in the hospital, but I still had not reached my ultimate high and was always chasing the next and greater high.

I was using so many drugs I no longer attempted to keep track of what or how many, and was shooting more and more alcohol into my veins as often as I could. I never thought about the consequences, nor did I even care.

Meanwhile, my fight against the infection continued. That summer, we thought we had defeated the infection and I attempted to return back to work. However, the infection returned a few weeks later and it was decided I should undergo several blood tests and a CT scan to see what was going on inside my spine. Just before sending me to have a CAT scan, my original surgeon and my wife thought it would be a good idea to do an x-ray of my back and stomach, to make sure I did not have any form of metal in me which would place me in danger during the CT scan.

The x-rays showed that when the doctor removed my spinal stimulator, he had decided to snip the wires and remove the spinal stimulator receiver, but leave the wire paddles that transferred the electrical stimulation to the spine, to reconnect at a later time. My surgeon was shocked to see the paddles in the x-rays and explained that when they left the metal paddles in my spine, they left me open for infection because the infection would attach itself to the foreign metal. We had an answer as to why I could not beat the infection. Needless to say, I was soon in surgery to have the remaining parts of the stimulator removed. After a short stay in the hospital, I was released to go home and a week later was released to return to work.

Although the infection mystery was cleared up, the addiction issue was now a huge problem I thought I could hide. From the day I returned to work, I was using on a regular basis. I hid pills, pain patches and even alcohol bottles in my desk, overhead bins and backpack I carried into work each day. I was using every chance I got and could not use enough.

My job required I travel from office to office, so I was trying to schedule my drug and alcohol use to the days I knew I did not have to travel. However, the addiction had become so severe by this point I became unconcerned about the days I had to travel and left it up to chance.

My boss and management team had been so supportive of me and here I was falling deeper and deeper into addiction. I would use before I left for work, use when I got to work, and continue to use throughout the day. I was searching out, finding, purchasing and redistributing drugs I had purchased on the street.

One day at work, my addiction was calling and I decided to use even more than I was used to. I grabbed one of my favorite orange bottles out of my backpack, removed the lid and dumped about twelve pills into the palm of my hand. I decided I needed more, so I tipped the bottle and dumped eight to ten more pills into my hand.

I swallowed the large amount of strong narcotics and took a swig of Diet Coke©. The effects of the pills took over and I was relaxed, numb and in another place. I was also attempting to do my job and had just printed off a report I had to retrieve from the fax machine. When I stood, the effects of the drugs multiplied and I could tell I had taken too many pills. As I walked, I swayed, the office seemed to be moving, and my vision appeared off. The fax machine appeared to be a few feet away to me, but in reality it was closer and I ran straight into it. Being the tall and large man I am, the sound of the impact was loud enough to gain the attention of my co-workers and boss, who had been walking by when this happened.

My boss had me in her office within minutes and spoke to me as if I were her own child, with love, respect and a deep concern. Although I was high, I realized I had let her down and figured my career was over, but what she decided shocked me.

"I know there is a great guy somewhere lost in this mess," she said after informing me of the severity of my actions. She leaned toward me in her chair. "I have faith you will find your way out of this endless maze and become the man I know you can be."

Instead of firing me right then and there, she told me she was going to send me to a local drug rehabilitation center and if I valued my job, I would take this offer seriously and not make light of it.

Two days after the fax machine incident, I was at a county run drug rehabilitation center only a few miles from where I lived. The first visit was to meet with a counselor for an initial assessment and to figure out which one of the programs would best fit my situation.

Even with the possibility of losing my job—the job I had wanted so bad, the job which was a big step in my becoming self-sufficient, and the job which could possibly lead to bigger and better things—I still wanted the drugs more. I attempted to stop using, but only made it a few hours before I gave in to the drugs again. I used right before meeting with this counselor, thinking it would make it easier and I would find it more comfortable to talk about my issues.

Looking back, that exact thought was my excuse for everything. Drugs would make it possible for me to do something and do it comfortably. Addiction consistently told me drugs were the answer to every problem I had, the pain I suffered, and life would not be possible without them. By now, drugs were not enough; I was also dependent on alcohol.

I took the powerful concoction and got into my car. This happened on a regular basis and I was under the influence of drugs and alcohol much of the time I was driving. Even worse, most of the time I was not alone in the car and had either my wife, children or worse yet, my grandson with me. I showed no regard for my passengers, or the other drivers I put in danger.

My appointment with the counselor at the outpatient drug rehabilitation clinic went just like every other initial assessment I had. I was asked questions and I answered them by telling the person what I thought he or she wanted to hear. The drugs and alcohol were definitely helping me get through the interview and they had a big investment on how successful the treatment was going to be. Addiction did not want me improving, it wanted me dead. It had me in its power, using before I sat down with the counselor, attempting to manipulate both the answers and the counselor, and doing whatever it took to get us out of the office and back to using.

For me, it was exhausting using drugs, manipulating, lying, remembering what I had said and to whom, hiding, stealing, buying, selling, and starting these actions over again and again. Every day was the same: live to use, use to live. Everywhere I went, I thought about using, making sure I had enough, getting what I needed, contacting those I could get it from, making doctor appointments where I thought I could score drugs, and having medical procedures just to get more drugs.

After answering questions for about ninety minutes, I was released to go home. Before I left, the counselor set me up to be a member of an addiction treatment group that met two nights a week. He felt this group would be a great fit for me due to several of the members suffering from similar addictions. He gave me a packet of information about the group, times I was expected to be there and a release paper stating I understood everything I heard in the group was confidential. I signed the release, took the packet and promised to be at the first meeting the next evening. Neither I, nor my addiction, had any intentions of stopping.

Addiction does not play fair and it does not care what or how much it costs you. My addiction had a stronghold on my life and I was ready and willing to sacrifice everything. I believed I could have everything, the job, family, success, happiness and the pills. I thought if I manipulated a little better and hid my using, I could continue to have it all. However, time would prove that was flawed thinking.

After work the following day, I reported to the rehabilitation center for my first group. I walked in and was greeted by the group counselor who introduced me to a few of the others and asked if I wanted a cup of coffee. I declined the coffee and took a seat next to a young lady who appeared to be in her late teens to early twenties. I struck up a conversation with her while a few others came in and took a seat.

I was in my early forties, wearing dress slacks, a white shirt and tie, and probably appeared to be your average run of the mill counselor or medical professional. The group I was part of that night was much younger and dressed in jeans, sweatshirts and tennis shoes. Although I may have looked like the leader, I was not one you would want to follow.

The first night of group was uncomfortable. The counselor had each of us introduce ourselves and give a brief synopsis of what brought us to the group and what we expected to get out of it. After listening to the others talk very little about their experiences and what they expected, I did not add much. I was embarrassed to be there and surely did not want to talk about how I got caught using at work and was sent here. I just shared I had a problem with pain medications.

This rehabilitation visit was my seventh and after a few months of attending and doing what they asked, I was released and sent on my way to be a successful individual in the game of life, as I had completed the group successfully.

Once again, I had manipulated and convinced others I was doing better, only to be living a life still in the turmoil and grips of addiction. I could talk the talk, act the way they wanted me to, manipulate my actions and behaviors, smile and talk with some sense, but I could not stop using.

Throughout this time my wife was working full time; my oldest son, Aaron, was married and had his son, Jayden; my son, Eric, graduated from high school, was attending the local community college and worked for an auto body repair shop; and my daughter, Sheri, was beginning her high school career and taking drivers training. Life was going on around me and I was in and out.

Who Is Ken?

I had improved my behaviors at work and had somewhat controlled my using. I appeared to be doing much better since attending the drug rehabilitation group and counseling. However, it was just smoke and mirrors, manipulation, scheduling and semantics. I was one person in one place and an entirely different person somewhere else.

I would work all day, go home, attempt to be interested in family events, and then go off alone to do things to feed my addiction. I would leave the house late at night and tell my wife I was going to go to the store just to pick up something and I would be right back. In reality, I was picking up drugs. By meeting others like myself in a parking lot, home, or park I could receive my most precious commodity.

Never in my wildest dreams would have I thought I would become a full blown drug addict. I was a man with an uncontrollable hunger and need for drugs and alcohol; a man out prowling around at night; a man who had given in to a disease that had the power and plan to end his life.

Ken Start was an addict. I could swallow countless pills, but the thought that I was an addict was hard to swallow. Therefore, I just continued to feed the addiction which allowed me some relief from the thoughts of my reality. If I spent my time chasing the next bigger and better high, I did not have to think about how I got to this point and what a mess my life had become.

As fall turned to winter and winter to spring of 2007, my life became more and more uncontrollable. To be truthful, it had become hell. I was using so much I couldn't get enough to feed my addiction. I was lying and manipulating everyone around me. I was severely depressed and had lost any glimmer of hope.

My back pain, the original and ever-present symptom, was taking much of my strength, especially after the loss of my electrical spinal stimulator. I was emotionally and physically weak, but my addiction was as strong as ever and I kept feeding it.

At work, I attempted to just lie low and fulfill my duties on a day-to-day basis. I knew I was in trouble; I knew I was running out of time and I believed I would either get fired or end up dead, whichever came first. I was playing Russian roulette with my job, family and life and the ammunition was drugs and alcohol. I hoped one of my high doses would shut down my body and I would fall asleep and not wake up, giving addiction the final victory and me death—the ultimate high.

It was at this time that my dad's health began to falter. He was a physical man, blue collar, self-made, workaholic, who was smart and could do just about anything with his two hands and intuition. He never graduated from high school, but was smarter than most men I knew. He now suffered from peripheral artery disease that had seriously affected his kidneys and circulation. His kidneys began to give out and his prognosis was he needed a new kidney, but for the time being, he was put on kidney dialysis. He also had to have a leg amputated due to poor circulation. We watched as he began his descent into serious illness, which was hard to witness.

He was always strong, outgoing, smart and one of those "larger than life" individuals. I was proud he went from quitting high school to owning his own successful business and becoming a local county commissioner for several years, never losing an election. I was, and still am, proud to be the son of Clarence Start.

Although our relationship was not super close, he had been there for me whenever I needed him. In fact, my relationship had become closer after my accident and addiction issues. My dad would have done anything to help me, but he was forced to stand helpless, not knowing what to do, which he was not used to.

He would call me three or four nights a week telling me everything would be okay. Just hearing that from my dad and knowing he had my back gave me some strength. However, even my dad's love and support could not pull me out of the grips of addiction. I continued to use and even used my dad's health as an excuse to use more. Using was more important than anything. It allowed me the escape from reality I thought I needed. My reality was depression, anxiety, doom, desperation, drugs, sickness, dread, regret and consuming pain.

In April 2007, I was working full time, but my pain and resulting addiction were both reaching their peaks. Consuming as many pills as I was, it was difficult to comprehend how my pain could be present, but it was worse than ever and I did not know what to do. I was high all the time, depressed beyond measure and losing whatever small amount of hope I had left.

Between Dr. Kaye's frustration and my wife's broken heart, it was decided I should make an appointment with Dr. Hooten at the Mayo Clinic.

Four days later, my wife, mother and I were sitting in Dr. Hooten's office, waiting for the man who had once helped me. I was nervous about seeing him.

When he walked in and looked at me, I immediately felt his genuine care and concern. He shook my hand, greeted my wife and mother and took a seat at his desk. After a few minutes of catching up and talking about general topics, Dr. Hooten looked at me and asked what it was that brought me to his office.

Looking back at him was one of the hardest things I ever had to do.

How Deep Is This Hole?

The last thing I wanted to do was let Dr. Hooten and the Mayo Clinic staff down, but I knew I had to come clean, or at least somewhat clean. With my wife and mother there I could not tell anyone what I was up to or how far I had fallen into the grips of addiction and negative behaviors.

Before I walked into his office, I had tried to build a reasonable explanation for what I had been through and how I was now sick, high and desperate. However, looking at Dr. Hooten, all the thoughts and ideas had vanished and I was left alone with nothing but the words that came out of my mouth.

While sharing everything I had been through since seeing him last, Dr. Hooten sat attentive, interested and engaged. He sat in his office chair leaning back slightly, wearing a dark blue suit, one leg crossed over the other and looking at me as though I was the only person in the world at that moment. I could feel his concern and knew he was listening to my every word. He never interrupted to ask questions or make comments, he was patient and waited until I was finished to ask questions and made it evident he had been listening the entire time.

While sharing, I relied heavily on my wife and mother to help me with dates and facts about each of the events. I told him how I had met with Patti M at Michigan Rehabilitation Services and followed their program in order to find full time employment. I informed him my auto insurance had recently appointed a case nurse, Patti W, who was assisting me and had been helpful.

I had so much to tell Dr. Hooten so he would understand how I had landed back in his office. I was nervous throughout the appointment, but Dr. Hooten had a calming effect on me. I knew I was not being judged or ridiculed for my actions and he would help me in any way possible.

After I shared my story, my wife and mother shared their view of where I was and where I was headed. Both of them cried throughout their recollections. While they spoke, I stared at the floor, wishing I had a handful of pills to swallow. It was hard knowing I was not doing well, but to hear it from others and know how my behaviors were hurting them was gut wrenching.

After listening, Dr. Hooten began reiterating some of the information to make sure he had heard it clearly and correctly. He also asked several questions about the medical surgeries and treatments I had since our last visit. Staying focused on me the entire time, Dr. Hooten then asked about the pain and how I was dealing with it. He asked about the medications I was taking and my wife gave him a list. However, it only had the prescribed medications and I was not ready to begin a conversation about just how bad the addiction had become and exactly how many and which drugs I was now taking.

Dr. Hooten felt the next best move would be for me to return to the Mayo Clinic Pain Rehabilitation Center, where he would be able to assist me in working on living with the pain. He was now the director of the clinic and felt it would help me by revisiting the coping skills for living with pain. It would also give him and his staff the opportunity to evaluate where I stood and what other medical or physical options may be possible through the Mayo Clinic.

Leaving his office, I felt some hope but also knew I had not been totally honest and transparent. My wife and mother had more hope leaving his office than I did. I knew I could come back and attend a three week outpatient clinic, manipulate my way through the experience and go home with the same problem. Addiction had no plans on letting go.

The moment I walked out of Dr. Hooten's office, I began strategizing how I was going to get through this clinic without their knowing the level of drugs I was taking, the alcohol I was shooting in my veins, and the activities I used to get the drugs I needed. My life was about manipulating so my addiction felt safe.

Addiction controlled my mind, body, thoughts, time, feelings, personality and every part of my being. It had me thinking about my drug or drugs of choice, from the time I woke to the moment I closed my eyes at night. Addiction controlled every waking moment and it could also affect my dreams. Almost every night, I would have dreams of using and the next and bigger high. Addiction became my god, promising salvation, happiness, acceptance, understanding and comfort from my ills.

Over the next two weeks, I tried to cut down on the amount of drugs I was taking. I knew I was going to be in an environment that did not support my addiction and had gone through withdrawal enough to know it was utter hell. I thought I could manipulate my circumstances so I could avoid some of the negative effects that stopping the high levels of drugs would cause and I was somewhat successful.

Over the few weeks before returning to the clinic, I cut down on the drugs I was self-prescribing, but I knew I was still taking too many and had to cut more. Days before traveling to Mayo for my second stint in the Pain Rehabilitation Center, I whittled away a few more pills and by the time I arrived at the clinic, I was taking much less than I had been taking a few weeks earlier.

I was still totally dependent on my own drugs, but I felt comfortable knowing if I had to cut more, I would not get as sick with withdrawal. I was about to learn I was very wrong.

Back to Mayo, Again

Two weeks later, I arrived in Rochester, Minnesota on July 4th. My wife had made my hotel arrangements and one of my friends drove me out there. He stayed one night and left early the next morning. I had to report to the Pain Rehabilitation Center that same morning, so after saying goodbye I walked the short distance from the hotel to the Pain Rehabilitation Clinic.

As I walked over to this familiar building, I was full of apprehension and regret. What was I doing? Did I want to do this? How did I let others talk me into this? I knew this stuff already. How would sitting through the next three weeks help me out? I was nervous about not being truthful with Dr. Hooten a few weeks ago. He was expecting me to revisit this information, go home and be revitalized, reinforced and ready for success. I thought I had suckered this intelligent man into believing my story. Although I felt somewhat guilty about manipulating Dr. Hooten, my addiction was more important and it was the only thing I had and I was holding onto it with all my might.

I thought Dr. Hooten had no idea I was coming back into his care with a larger than expected addiction issue. I knew my acting had just begun and it was time to lay it on thick. I had to outsmart Dr. Hooten, the man who was trying to help me.

I reported to the receptionist and she remembered me from my earlier visit. After chatting for a few moments, she had me take a seat in the community room where she informed me my preselected nurse case manager would meet with me and assist me in getting started with the paperwork.

I had only been sitting in the community room for a short time, when a smiling and cheery nurse came out and introduced herself as Sue V. I remembered seeing her at my first visit, but had never met or spoken with her one-on-one. Sue asked me to follow her to her office and the entire time we walked, she made me feel welcome.

Once in her office, she had me take a seat in a chair next to her desk. After a few minutes of chatting and asking about my trip out to Mayo, Sue shared she had spoken with Dr. Hooten and he informed her of my current situation. She smiled and congratulated me on the success I had earned after my first visit here, never mentioning the new injury or conditions. She said she was so glad I had made the choice to come back and go through the program again.

I responded that returning made me feel like a failure. Sue shared I was not the first one to return for a second visit and I surely would not be the last. She gave me credit for doing what was best for me. Sue also brought up the fact that a new injury as severe as mine often rocked people's recovery and the best thing to do was ask for help.

She went through the required paperwork, informing me of my selected group and schedule, rules for participation, medication list and schedule, and then supplied me with a huge three ringed binder which held the curriculum for the entire three week clinic and several other important items. She took my vitals, current weight and asked several medical questions. Before leaving her office, she had me fill out a few questionnaires concerning my pain levels, depression and anxiety levels, as well as other physical and mental health issues the program used to assess improvement, risks, problem areas and things I needed to work on while in the program.

After about an hour or so, Sue said it was time for me to get started and brought me to the room where my assigned group was meeting. The Pain Rehabilitation Clinic had two separate groups, both were pain related but had to be separated due to size. The smaller sized groups allowed more intimacy and one-on-one communication.

The door to the room was closed and it was obvious the group was in session. Sue knocked and the leader of this group, Sue B, another RN case worker, certified in working with groups and patients dealing with chronic pain issues, came to the door. She greeted me with a warm hand shake and kind hello. I remembered her from my first visit and she remembered me, too.

Sue B directed me in choosing a seat at one of the five circle tables in the room. After selecting a seat in the back of the room, Sue B introduced me to my new group. I was feeling the lack of drugs and comfort they supplied. Up to this point, I had been feeling pretty good because I had taken pills before walking over to the clinic.

As Sue B was saying my name, I began to sweat and feel clammy due to nerves, doubt, regret and feeling uncomfortable. I smiled, nodded my head and even said thank you for having me. Inside, I was feeling my normal sense of regret and a wave of remorse flowed over me.

Sue B. then had the rest of the group introduce themselves and one by one they each said their name and where they were from. In this semi-small group of about 13 people, we hailed from all over the United States and even one from Canada.

While the others were introducing themselves, I was thinking about my next opportunity to use. I was running on low, just like a smoker who needed a cigarette, I needed my next high. If I could use, then I could calm down, fit in better and be able to disguise my addiction better. I was also thinking about where I could use in the facility.

I decided I would go to the restroom and take one of my self-prescribed doses. Sue B stated we would take a ten minute break, come back and pick up from where we left off.

After a few hellos, I slipped away and found the nearest restroom where I swallowed some pills, not as many as I was used to, but enough to take the edge off. This would be my routine for the next few days.

As I became more familiar with the schedule and the others in my group, I continued to plan my time so I could use and not be noticed. I also became more and more involved in the pain management clinic's schedule. They kept us busy and each moment was carefully planned to assist us in living with the pain that had brought us there.

Some people in my group were there for back, neck, arm or leg pain. Others were there for head pain, including different types of headaches, and some were there for fibromyalgia, and various failed surgeries. Each of us came at different times, as the clinic rotated new patients in and out. None of us started together, which allowed us the opportunity to witness the frustration, sense of defeat, different levels of pain behaviors, depression and anxious moods of some of the patients coming in. We also witnessed the hope for the future of those who were graduating and looking forward to their new lives.

The Pain Rehabilitation Center provided many types of treatments and therapies in an integrated program, to help each of us achieve our individual rehabilitation goals. My group leader, along with the assistance of other medical professionals at the clinic, used core components such as Medication Management, Chemical Health Education, Stress Management and Relaxation, Physical Therapy, Occupational and Recreational Therapy, Biofeedback, Sleep, Hygiene and Lifestyle Management, in order to have each of their patients complete a multi-disciplinary program.

The clinic used the different aspects of rehabilitation to help us with returning to regular day activities, increasing physical strength, reducing pain medications, learning stress management techniques, returning to gainful employment, resuming leisure and recreational activities, improving interpersonal relationships, reducing reliance on health-care professionals and improved ability to self-manage chronic pain.

Making the decision to participate in the Pain Rehab Center was challenging, not easy, and took a large commitment from not only the PRC staff, but the patient as well. Before starting the program, we had to ask these questions:

- Is my life focused on pain and what I am able to do, rather than, what I am able to do in spite of pain?
- Are my doctors telling me there is nothing further they can do to relieve the pain?
- Do they tell me I need to learn to get on with my life?
- Am I truly concerned about the long-term effects of taking pain medications?
- Is my family's well-being affected because of my chronic pain?

- Is my recovery from injury or illness taking much longer than my doctors or I expected?
- Am I not able to commit to social events with family or friends because my pain may be higher that day?

I did not want to give up the drugs. What kind of mess had I gotten myself into and how was I going to manipulate my way out of it?

I attended every session, took notes, participated, made new friends and even enjoyed some of it, but had no intentions of giving up my drugs. My addiction had no intentions of letting me go, either.

The Truth

While attending the clinic's three week outpatient pain program, I was staying at a local hotel where I made new friends not associated with the Mayo Clinic. Some of the friends were great people and some were not such great influences.

Two people I got to know were staff members at the hotel. These two individuals, without knowing it, assisted in keeping my mood up by taking time out of their schedules to chat with me, smile and share a laugh.

I also learned how to get what I wanted in this small town by using some of the same skills I had learned and honed back home. Before I knew it, I was active in getting drugs from people I never thought I would associate with.

Three days before I was scheduled to leave the Pain Rehabilitation Center, I was called to meet with one of the head nurses, Joan, who worked alongside Dr. Hooten and was present in every meeting I had with him. As soon as I heard about the appointment, warning flags went off in my head, not just warning flags, but ear-busting, loud sirens.

Although I was worried, I knew Joan and that gave me some comfort. Joan was not just one of the head nurses, she taught certain topics during the program and was a great teacher with a warm heart and smile. During my first visit, my wife and parents traveled from Michigan to attend the day long family portion of the program that taught family members how to assist patients in the difficult task of being successful when they were sent home. During that program, my dad fell in love with Joan and her gentle, sincere, professional and caring manner. She was the staff member my father always asked about, since she had left such a positive and lasting impression on him.

My appointment took place less than an hour after my last self-prescribed dose of drugs, so I was feeling some comfort from the handful of pills. However, I was still nervous about what Joan and I were going to talk about. Would we talk about my progress, my work situation, my marriage or my family issues? Or maybe it was about how far I had come in the program. I didn't know, but I was thankful I had some support from the pills. In fact, just before I was to meet with Joan, I decided a little back-up would be good, so I took a walk to the restroom and swallowed a few extra.

Joan found me in the community room and we walked the short distance to her office. Right from the start, she kept talking to me and helped me relax. As I sat in a chair and made small talk, I looked around her office and saw several pictures of her family members. I thought how blessed they were to have such a great mother. I was feeling a small buzz at the time and knew I could expect a bit more support in a few minutes.

Joan did not waste any time getting to the point. She, Dr. Hooten and the team felt it would be beneficial for me to stay a few extra days. She explained that I was doing a great job, but they felt I would benefit from a longer stay.

My heart about dropped to the floor. Why did they think I should stay? Why didn't they think others should stay? What had I done that made me a weaker individual? How did this happen? I thought I was doing so good at acting, making it look as though I was taking it in, asking the right questions, saying the right things and appearing to be the star pupil. Apparently I was wrong.

Joan then looked at me and said she felt there was more to my situation than I was letting on. She leaned toward me and said I should think about getting help with my addiction issue. My first thought was that I didn't have an addiction issue.

Numb from Joan's words, but with a smile on my face, I did not know how to react. At this point, she turned to her desk and picked up a blue folder containing information about the Mayo Clinic Addiction Services Center.

Rehabilitation
Home Away from Home

I woke the next morning in my clothes knowing I had used too much the night before. I showered, changed into clean clothes and left my hotel room, headed to the Pain Rehabilitation Clinic for another day of learning, participating and pretending.

On my walk over, I took a few pills to ready myself for another day. As I walked over, I relived the conversation I had had with Joan less than twenty-fours earlier. She had mentioned I should contact my wife and family to see what they thought of having me attend the Mayo Clinic Addictions Service Center and that Dr. Hooten was going to talk to me about the addiction program. Now I was to meet with Dr. Hooten in just an hour or so.

I went through the morning routine at the clinic with my classmates. I made goals for the day. I went to the morning stretch exercises. I reviewed my schedule and I shared my previous night at the hotel. I could not tell the truth, so I made it sound as though I had a great evening—a walk, quiet dinner, movie and bed at a healthy time. However, my reality was much different. Matter of fact, I was still physically experiencing the effects of the heavy amount of drugs I had taken just to deal with the conversation with Joan. I was feeling lifeless, numb, cloudy and disappointed in myself.

However, my addiction was telling me I had to take more pills.

Before I knew it, I was in the board room with Sue V, Sue B, Joan and Dr. Hooten. He started by asking me how things were going with the program, what concerns I had at the time, what my successes and struggles were, and how I was feeling physically with the medication tapering off. As always, he was cool and calm and I was a mess inside. While he was talking and asking me questions, I wanted to run, but it would blow my cover and then they would know who I really was.

I struggled to answer the questions Dr. Hooten had asked, but all I could think about was when and how he would bring up the question about the inpatient addiction clinic. Finally, Dr. Hooten asked me about the conversation I had had with Joan the previous day.

The actor in me came out and played the role of wanting the help and appreciating all they were doing for me. I stated Joan had been great and I felt she hit the nail on the head with her judgment of my trouble with addiction. I went on and on as if I totally agreed with Joan, Dr. Hooten and the rest of the clinic. Of course, I had the help and support of the drugs I had taken earlier, but I am sure I sounded like I wanted nothing more than to sign right up for the addiction clinic and would do my best to succeed.

I don't remember what Dr. Hooten's initial response was, or what the response of the team in the room was, but I knew I had just survived an interview and assessment I was dreading. However, the satisfaction of knowing I had survived the interview only lasted minutes when I realized I had agreed with everything they had suggested. Now what was I going to do? My addiction was not ready to give up and go away, just because I was going to another rehab.

Now the other Ken came out to play. This was the addict who would do anything to hold on and survive. My addiction went into survival mode and shifted from doing what was asked of me, to what was I going to have to do to manipulate my way out of this mess.

The rest of the day I stayed focused on how I could manipulate this situation to please them and myself. I created several different plans in my head while attending the groups, physical therapy and other activities required.

Shortly before being released for the day, Joan pulled me aside and informed me they were beginning the process of admitting me into the inpatient addiction clinic. As I walked back to the hotel, I was a total mess. I had all but successfully completed the Pain Rehabilitation Center and felt I had a good grip on how I could go home and successfully live with the chronic pain. I wanted to work, spend time with family and friends and participate in leisure activities. I wanted to feel better about myself, have a schedule, make goals and be a responsible individual. I did not want to give up the drugs in order to do this.

When I arrived back at my hotel room, I made the call to my wife and shared with her the plan. She was supportive right from the start. Why wouldn't she be? After my call home, I sat on the bench outside the hotel and thought about the predicament I was in. What would I do? Would I finally make the right choice? Would I let everyone down again? Rehab number eight. What would make this one any different? Tears of fear ran down my face. This was real fear, inner fear, and fear of the unknown, fear of life without drugs, fear of trying and fear of failing.

A Dark Cloud

After a night of thinking about the likelihood of another inpatient drug rehab, using to fall asleep, and waking up feeling worse than when I fell asleep, I showered, dressed and walked to the Pain Rehabilitation Center for another day of pretending.

Now my nurse case worker Patti W, representing my no-fault auto insurance from the accident, was involved and she was communicating with both the Mayo Clinic and my insurance adjuster. Patti W had contacted the auto insurance and they rejected the idea of me attending yet another drug and alcohol rehabilitation program. The adjuster shared with Patti W that they had given up on me succeeding and felt they had paid for enough drug rehabilitation programs in the past. Although Patti W knew about my past stints in several drug rehabilitation programs, she believed that, with the momentum from the pain clinic, I had a shot at success in this drug and alcohol clinic.

Patti W went to bat for me behind the scenes, with the adjuster from my auto insurance. She made the argument that with my current documented success with the pain program, along with Dr. Hooten's blessing and referral, it would be foolish to send me home and set up for failure. She added that the Mayo Clinic was one of the best, I was already here, and the opportunity was created for me to attend one of the best substance abuse programs around. After making a solid case on my behalf, the insurance company changed their opinion and decided to approve my stay at the Mayo Clinic drug rehabilitation program.

I only had two days left at the Pain Rehabilitation Center. I attempted to stay focused on the information I was learning, but my addiction would not allow me to focus on anything other than the decision that I attend the drug rehab clinic.

So what does an addict do when he or she has to deal with a difficult situation? They use. I left the pain rehab unit, walked to the local park where I had met some people, and purchased some old friends in an orange bottle.

That night, on the eve of my graduation from the pain clinic, my group of classmates planned a graduation dinner at a local restaurant. Laughing and giggling with my class-mates, I attended the dinner high the entire time. Later, alone in my hotel, the laughing and giggling ended. I did not have to pretend when alone in my room. Instead, I stared at the ceiling, confused, scared and frustrated.

The next morning I was sad knowing I would leave the friends I had made and the clinic where I felt at home, for a new clinic and a new experience. The most upsetting concept for me was I had been able to use on a limited level at the pain rehab clinic, but at a drug rehab clinic, I knew I would not get away with using.

My last day started with making daily goals, exercis-ing, attending lecture groups and physical therapy. I laughed with the group, as if everything was great. I smiled as if I had plans of returning home, changing my lifestyle into a new and revitalized way of living, and using the tools I had gained while attending the pain rehab clinic.

I met with Dr. Hooten and together, with the regular team in the board room, he congratulated me on making it through the Pain Rehabilitation Center for my second time and making the decision to follow through with the drug rehab clinic. He also stated, by having that piece to add to the puzzle, I would be able to create a life that would bring stability and success. Dr. Hooten, along with some of the others, shared they believed in me and that I had what it took to take control of my life and make it what I wanted it to be. The one thing that stood out from the meeting was when Dr. Hooten said he would be there when I completed the drug rehab unit. In addition, Michelle, another RN case manager, stated I was welcome to attend the Pain Management Aftercare Sessions she led once or twice a month.

Although I felt anxious about the drug rehabilitation clinic, I left the meeting feeling the team would be there for me if, and when, I needed them. I was also excited about the aftercare as I had never attended a program where they stayed in touch.

I left the Pain Rehabilitation Center with a new sense of revitalization and even though I was using throughout the program, I had given up quite a bit. I had binged a few times, but I did attempt to control my intake of drugs so I didn't feel the uncomfortable side effects of withdrawal. I also left the program a healthier individual. I was walking five miles every day, stretching, biking, working out, participating in yoga, meditating, learning to set achievable and attainable goals, setting a schedule, and being accountable for my time. I had also learned how to plan for a bad day, participate in family events and enjoy each moment for what it was.

However, even though I had found success, I still had the dark cloud that followed me everywhere. My addiction was still more important than the success I had found. My chances of going home and keeping the momentum going from the Pain Rehabilitation Center with my current addiction was zero. I wanted to just get home and use on my own schedule again. Addiction was waiting for me with wide open arms and all its deceitful, manipulating and deadly attributes.

Anxiety With A Capital "A"

After saying good bye to my classmates and leaving the Pain Rehabilitation Center, I walked to the hotel where I would spend one last night before being admitted into the inpatient drug rehabilitation unit. My wife and daughter-in-law had driven from Michigan to spend the night with me and assist me in the transition.

When I arrived at the hotel, I was met by my wife and daughter-in-law. I was glad to see them, but I had gotten used my freedom and with others there I lost some of that freedom. However, we did enjoy a nice dinner at a local restaurant and then went out to purchase some new clothes, snacks, books, and some personal items. We returned to the hotel room, used the laundry facilities, and then packed my bags in preparation for my admittance into the drug rehab clinic the next day.

I didn't sleep, as I was anxious about the transition about to take place. I was also anxious about losing my freedom to come and go as I pleased, to return to my room each night, to do what I wanted and go where I wanted. I didn't want to lose the control of using when and where I wanted. In reality, I could think of nothing else.

A few times throughout the night, I wanted to scream. So many things were running through my mind—losing my freedom, losing control, meeting new people, wanting to get better, not wanting to give up drugs, wanting to tell the truth, worrying about how I could manipulate the new people, what was I going to do, and how was I going to get myself out of this mess.

In the morning, the three of us showered, dressed and ate breakfast at the hotel. Afterward we gathered my items, packed them into the car and drove over to the Mayo Clinic.

After reporting to the office, they provided me with paperwork which I completed and handed back. I was then told one of the team members from the addiction clinic would be coming soon to take me to my assigned room.

Although it only took a team member a few short minutes to come, it seemed like an eternity. I sat there in the small waiting room and felt like I was going to have a panic attack. I was sitting between my wife and daughter-in-law, yet I still felt alone and vulnerable. It was a good thing I had taken a self-prescribed cocktail of pills before having breakfast. It was the only thing that got me through. My mind was running faster and faster, telling me to get up and run anywhere but here.

A woman came in with a bright smile on her face and asked if I was Ken. She sat down next to us and greeted my wife, daughter-in-law and me with a warm welcome. After a few minutes of talking to the three of us about where we were from, my wife and daughter-in-law's trip here, and my children and grandchild, she asked me to follow her. We went to her office where we could talk in more detail about the program and what I could expect. A few hours later, I was sitting in my assigned group and my wife and daughter-in-law were on their way back to Michigan.

Before I knew it, I was meeting my new classmates, most of them were not dealing with physical pain like my former classmates. These individuals were dealing with the emotional and mental pain of deadly addictions to alcohol and drugs.

My counselor, Tom, asked me to introduce myself. He did not have me go into detail about my life, medical issues or addiction, he just had me tell the group where I was from and what I was addicted to. After sharing, Tom had the group introduce themselves by name and what drug had brought each member there. Afterward, Tom said he would have me introduce myself in more detail later.

Tom clearly knew what he was doing and how to allow an individual to settle in and get acquainted with the routine. For that, I was thankful. However, it soon became apparent Tom was not there to mess around and this group was meant for those serious about working toward becoming clean.

In my first group, I listened to a classmate tell his story about using alcohol, hiding his use, manipulating and how his addiction had taken control of his life. I was immediately able to relate. As he went on, he shared how he drank several bottles of hard liquor a day and since he lived on a farm, he would hide the glass bottles by throwing them in an unused farm silo.

The further he went with his story the more I related. He was a married college professor, a father and grandfather. He told us how the alcohol took control and his drinking was more important than anything else in his life. He also shared how he had become the master of manipulation and had obsessed about how and when he could use and hide his using.

The more he talked, the more I related. However, I was more addicted to drugs than I was alcohol. I had to have my drugs. The alcohol I shot into my veins was just used to increase the intensity of the drugs. I had been in Rochester attending the pain rehab clinic for over a month and had not shot up or drunk alcohol. However, I had used drugs that morning.

I would learn a drug is a drug, be it prescription drugs, meth, street drugs, wine, champagne or alcohol. I listened to this man talk about his struggles with alcohol and over the next two weeks, I would hear stories of each of the others. Each of them had at least one thing in common with me, addiction. As I listened to their stories, I heard countless similarities with addiction, unmanageable lives, marriage issues, health issues, honesty, integrity problems, job issues and relationship problems with spouses, children, friends, and generally everyone around them.

Although I listened and could relate to each of their stories, I did not buy into the rehab itself. I made friends with my new classmates in the first few days, liked them and knew I had things in common, but felt they were far worse and further along in their addictions than me. I was shocked and saddened to hear how far each of their addictions had taken them from their families, careers, friends and life.

For the first two weeks, I shared my story and how addiction had interrupted my life. I listened to the others, spent time with them, but did not work on myself. I shared what I thought they wanted to hear, and spit out answers to the questions Tom asked of me. I attended each of the scheduled groups, ward activities, meals, doctor's appointments and AA meetings I was asked to attend off campus. I did the random drug testing they asked me to do. The moment I walked in the doors of the drug rehab clinic the first day, I quit using everything except what was prescribed for me. All I took was blood pressure medication and another medication meant for my mood and pain.

In my reality, I thought I was pulling off the big scam by doing just enough to get by, smiling, listening, participating, shedding a few tears and making friends. I thought it was going great. I listened to stories and even gave input on how they could better their lives. I went to the AA meetings and was nervous to talk, but did my best when it was my turn to say something. One time I became so nervous, I forgot my name so I just sat there looking at the others in the circle and smiled.

It was quite a shock to me, almost three weeks into my rehab stay, when Tom asked if he could speak to me after group. He told me I was wasting my time in the unit and asked if I was there to get help or just manipulate my way back home so I could die in my addiction. Tom asked me if I wanted to stay and get serious, or if I wanted to return home.

For me and my addiction, it was a no-brainer. We wanted to go home. After stating I would be better going home, Tom said he would set up a phone appointment with my wife, himself and me.

Later in the day, I found myself sitting in Tom's office having a three way phone conversation. Tom shared with my wife how the inpatient rehab stay had been going thus far; how I was listening, talking and making friends with the others, but I was not working on myself or my addiction issues. He told my wife I had two options: one was buying into the program and deciding my life was worth it and the other was to finish out the next two days, leave and return home.

Tom asked me to tell my wife which option I had elected. Being the fake I was, in a happy manner I stated I had elected for option two. I expected to hear my wife say she would make arrangements to come and get me.

There was a long silence, a bit of static and Tom looking at me.

"I love you dearly," my wife said, "but if you decide to leave the great facility you are blessed to be in, you will have to find another home." She went on to say she had decided she and my children deserved and needed me to come home healthier, with tools to be able to work on the addiction and start rebuilding our lives.

> *Sheryl – For years I had made excuses for Ken, until his rehab at Mayo Clinic in 2007. His counselor called me at home and asked, "Will Ken be able to come home if he doesn't want to stay at the addiction clinic?" It was the hardest thing I had to decide, but I had had enough of the excuses and defending Ken the addict. I loved him. I needed him. Our children needed him. But we needed him clean, sober, alert and involved. I just couldn't continue anymore with him as an addict. Sobbing and with my heart broken, I made the hardest decision. If he didn't stay and get the help he needed, he did not have a place in our home anymore.*

What had just happened? I was so used to being able to manipulate people and situations, I had not even thought about this not going my way. I was shocked and I panicked after hearing my wife share I would have to find another home if I did not stay and get the help I needed.

After the conversation, Tom shared with both my wife and me that he would give me a day or two to think about my options. Now what? That night I did not smile or laugh with the others. I did not listen to anyone in group. I did not participate and I did not feel like doing anything. All I could think about was whether I did or did not want to get better. I felt so confused, frustrated and lost. I was walking around as if I was in another world and this time, the other world did not include the effects of drugs.

I spent most of my time in my room with the door closed. I laid on my bed trying to find myself, my real self, and attempting to figure out what it was I truly wanted. Did I want to stay sick, addicted, unreliable, undependable, sad, depressed and suicidal? Or did I want to give recovery a real try? It sounded like an easy decision, but it wasn't.

I had never bought into the recovery path, nor did I ever have any sobriety I could speak of. Therefore, my self-confidence about this new option of recovery was not encouraging. I laid in my bed thinking about what would make this time any different. How would I succeed? Who would be there when I returned home to help me? What if I used again as I knew I would.

I thought about my wife, parents, children, family and friends. I thought about my job, knowing if I didn't do something, my boss was going to unplug my chances at a future with the organization. My faith also played a role. I believed in a God who created me for bigger and better things. He had a plan for me and I was definitely not following the instructions He had laid out for me to be successful.

I did more soul searching than I had ever done before. I prayed. I walked around my room, listened to music, prayed more and stared at the ceiling. During attempts to become sober in my past, I had heard that when I had a decision to make, I should play the results in my mind like a video. Playing the going home option was much more comforting with no problems, no worries, no effort, no change and no future. The mind video, of the staying option, was scary as hell with having to try, chances at failure, and giving up things I truly loved. I would also have to show responsibility, step up to the plate, and be dependable, trustworthy and consistent. Watching those around me smile, pat me on the back, support me and see myself with family, friends, co-workers and others while living a successful life, almost gave me the chills. After watching both mental visuals in my head and knowing which decision would lead to more happiness for me and those around me, I fell asleep.

When I awoke the next morning, after only an hour or two of sleep, I was reminded of the decision I had to make. I showered, shaved and got dressed. I went out to the community room and ate breakfast with my friends, and then went to our normal morning group. Little did I know, this day in rehab would be different from any other day I had spent in rehabs in the past and I would be presented with information that would change my life forever.

My New Plan

The next morning, as the group began to filter into the small therapy room, we noticed Tom had written information on the white board on the wall. He had never used the white board before, so everyone in the room questioned his agenda.

Down one side of the white board were several numbers. None of us knew what these numbers were for or what they represented, but we knew they had some significance since Tom had taken the time to write them on the board. It wouldn't be long before we learned what they meant and how they related to group, and especially me.

Tom came in and, as usual, took time to check in with each of us and see how our evenings went the night before. He then announced he had something different planned. He stated the numbers written on the board represented the visits I had with multiple drug rehabilitation units in the past fifteen years. To say the least, he had my attention.

The list of numbers started on the top of the left side and descended down, taking up most of the left side of the board. Tom went on to say that his plan for group was to do an autopsy of my attempts at recovery and past drug rehab visits.

He then walked up to the white board and started with the first number 92, which stood for 1992 and my first stay in a recovery facility. He wrote down the name of the facility, the length of time I spent there, what type of treatment, and how long I remained sober after I left. Along with the information I gave him, he had some of his own.

As Tom went through the list, number by number, year by year, treatment by treatment, failure by failure, I became aware of the time, resources, money and happiness I had wasted. It was evident that others, including my family, friends, and doctors, had attempted to get me help and do their best at aiding me by trying to lift me out of the depression, anxiety and addiction I was drowning in.

I had gone to each of these rehab visits knowing I was only doing it to make others happy and buy some time. These visits had become learning sessions where I listened to other abusers and learned new things from their personal experiences. I then incorporated some of those behaviors as my own.

I had never voluntarily, or for any other reason, gone to a rehab facility with the thought, or goal, of giving up my drugs, alcohol or addiction. I had struggled with the thoughts of wanting to be clean and healthy, but the thoughts of using were stronger, more familiar and more inviting. Addiction was a friend. It was dependable, always there and willing to help me whenever I needed it.

I had proven I could not keep myself clean and sober for any length of time, without running back to the drugs and sense of comfort they provided. As Tom continued and I listened to this autopsy of my treatment plans, I was hit hard with my sad reality. After lying in bed the previous night, wrestling with the thoughts of the conversation with my wife, knowing I had a decision to make and now seeing my treatment history in black and white, I knew I could not continue acting and behaving as if I did not have options.

After the group session, we had a break and then came back to the room to focus on a new topic. I was still focused on my situation, my options and my decision. While attending the group session, we had our scheduled lunch. While the others went to lunch, I took a long walk outside. Alone with my thoughts, I walked through the city of Rochester, thinking about the scary prospect of giving up the drugs, the addiction, the power, and the control. Could I trust this facility to aid me in finding success once and for all?

As I walked, I thought about the time I had wasted and could never regain; and the money I had thrown down the drain and would never get back. I thought about my wife, children, parents, employers and friends and how I had manipulated, lied, stolen and behaved in a detestable manner.

I was attempting to buy into rehab and see what recovery might hold for me. It was not an easy picture to see, but I was beginning to put the pieces of the puzzle together and with the assistance of the Mayo Clinic, beginning to truly see for the first time that I might have a chance at success.

I went back to group with my classmates and listened intently to the others. This time I listened with care and concern and with an open mind and heart.

I made the decision to change my life that day. I decided to take a chance, trust my faith, believe Tom and allow him and the other medical professionals to assist me in fighting my battle with addiction.

For the first time, I was going to let others in. I was going to let others know about the demons I was battling on a regular basis and allow others to work alongside me in learning a new way of life.

This was brand new territory for me and I was terrified. I was two or three weeks into the present treatment and had been away from home for almost two months.

In the next few days, I shared with Tom, the groups, the attending physician and other medical professionals, the depth and reality of my addiction. I shared the true amounts of my using, the severity of mixing different drugs, the reality of buying and selling drugs to get what I needed, and the shooting of alcohol into my veins.

I attempted to be honest, something I had not done in many years. I also attempted to be transparent, to let others see what I was truly dealing with. I opened up about my addiction, failures, family, work, dreams and hopes and laid my cards on the table for the first time.

Over the next few days, Tom worked with me and gave me a plan with different steps to assist me with success. Some of these steps were to attend AA meetings regularly in Rochester whenever possible, contact a person I thought might be a good candidate for a sponsor back home in Michigan, and find someone back home who would get rid of the drugs and alcohol I had hidden around the house.

Along with participating in the groups, buying into rehab, being honest and transparent, I made the call to a friend back home to clean out my drugs and alcohol. I attended every AA meeting I could, riding the little bus the recovery unit provided for transportation. I started taking the AA meetings much more seriously and began sharing and being open and honest at the meetings.

Selecting a sponsor was a bigger process. I hated asking for help, and hated the thought of telling someone else about my addiction. I was wrestling with the old thought that if I told someone else, it would be another individual I would have to be accountable to. I was an addict, I didn't like being accountable, dependable and or confronted. For me to want a person to do all that was hard, but I knew if Tom said it was necessary, I needed to do it.

Within two days, I had prayed about it, talked to Tom, and decided to call a man I respected and considered a friend back home. However, I was worried about rejection, embarrassment and being uncomfortable. I was sitting in group when Tom asked if I had called the gentleman I had selected to ask.

"Not yet," I said.

"There's no time like the present," he said and asked me to leave the room, call him and then return to group and share what I had learned.

My heart sank, but I walked out of the room and made the call. Dan Wright was a friend back home who was active in the recovery community and was understanding, comical and devoted to his recovery. I dialed his number and hearing the phone ring, my mouth went dry and my heart sank.

"Hello," Dan said. After we spoke for a few moments about life in general, my health and addiction issues, I asked if he would be my sponsor when I returned home.

Dan accepted the responsibility and we talked for a few more minutes about when I might come home. He suggested that when I got closer to returning home I should call him and we would make a plan. We said our goodbyes and hung up. My happiness slipped from ecstatic to dread within seconds of hanging up the phone. What had I done? Now there was someone else who would know about my battles, weaknesses, and flaws and require me to be responsible and successful.

My addiction was screaming as it did not want to let go just because I made a decision to give recovery a try. With every positive decision I made in the direction of recovery, my addiction was there to let me know it would never work. My addiction spoke to me every day. It would place the words 'regret' and 'defeat' into my mind and want nothing more than for me to fail. My addiction was not going to lie down and surrender on its own or willingly.

Stinking Thinking

I never saw or expected my addiction to return, knock me over and slam me upside the head so fast.

Over the past few days I had struggled, wrestled and dealt with making the decision to turn my life around. I had prayed, spent time alone and cried, talked with others, opened up in group, listened and prayed more. In the end, I made the decision to give recovery a try.

In my mind, it was over and I would never use again. I had bought into the whole program. It was like one of the diets I had tried in the past. You know how you plan, but keep putting it off until a specific start date, and then that date comes and you reset the start date. When you finally start, you decide to never cheat and only eat healthy foods. No more shakes and burgers, only celery, carrots and water with lemon. That is how my mind took on this recovery. I would never use again. My days with drugs were over. I was a new man and could not reset the start date.

I had done a lot of work already. I had made the huge decision to jump into recovery, opened up and found a sponsor, was reading my 12-step literature, went to meetings, shared at meetings, listened at meetings, and carried a list of phone numbers given to me from others in the 12-step program. I was good to go. I was taking it one day at a time and thought that since I was pretty competitive in spirit, I would once and for all nip this addiction in the bud. I saw great things in my future - better relationships, integrity, trust, health, a successful and fulfilling career, and a drug free life.

Three or four days into my 'ultimate recovery,' a friend from rehab and I decided to take a walk. We were both addicts, but I was in recovery and he was too, so we could safely talk about drugs. As we walked together that warm and humid Minnesota afternoon, we got onto the topic of using. Imagine. Two addicts talking about drugs. Before I knew it, we were in the grocery store buying aerosol cans of whipped cream and a large bag of party balloons. My buddy knew a way we could use and not have it be found in our urine tests. Well, forget recovery, like two clowns at the circus we were acting foolishly and before I knew it I was behind the grocery store sitting on a picnic table huffing and getting high.

I had made the decision just days earlier and thought I had put this drug nonsense behind me. Wrong! I had never done huffing before and I probably did not do it correctly, but all I felt when we finished was an aching headache. As an addict this was a huge disappointment. We laughed and joked about what we thought we had gotten away with on our walk back to the rehab unit, but I knew I had messed up.

Although my addiction was thrilled, I had enough sense from the past few days to know I had done something stupid. My addiction was yelling regret and defeat to me later as I lay in bed, alone in my room. No blood or urine test was needed for me to feel like a loser once again. My addiction and sick thinking tried to step in and regain control. Addiction and stinking thinking was what I was used to and comfortable with. But I remembered something from a 12-step meeting that day, "If I wanted something that I had never had, I would have to try something I had never tried."

I knew that after the foolish activity I had taken part in that day, I was only setting myself up for the same old routine of regret and defeat. I wanted better things for myself. I had to stop embracing addiction and try something new. That something new was recovery.

Although addiction attempted to regain control, I was ready and willing to try something new. Don't think for a minute I did this with a smile on my face or a song in my heart. I did it because I trusted those around me who were speaking sense and attempting to reach out to me. For some unknown reason, I was giving in to recovery.

Huffing in the back of a grocery store was the last time I used a drug of any sort. After realizing recovery was my number one priority and full-time job and career, I moved on and followed the rehab program, its philosophy, instructions and rules.

Over the next two or three weeks I did everything asked of me. Between the groups, exercising daily, 12-step meetings and with the help of Tom, I slowly built my treatment team back home.

I was still struggling, though. Not with my decision to participate in recovery, but in the fact I was realizing just how bad I had screwed up, wasted so many years and hurt so many people. It took the love, support and friendship of my counselor, medical team and my classmates there at Mayo to help me put it into perspective. I still had time to turn this ship around and sail into a safe harbor.

One evening during my last week of inpatient care in the rehab unit, I took a walk. I walked every day, but this time I decided to walk in the early evening. It was almost dark and I could see a thunderstorm coming in from the west. I took off wearing my exercise clothes with my music buds in my ears, knowing I was going to graduate and be released to outpatient care in just a few days.

As I walked I listened to music, I contemplated what my life may be like back at home. Could I really succeed at this recovery? Would this truly be my recovery? Before I knew it, I was downtown Rochester, MN amid the tall buildings of the Mayo Clinic and it began to rain.

Rain doesn't describe it. The skies opened up and I was soaked. Usually, I would not want to get drenched, but that night was different for me. I felt I had a cleansing moment and almost danced in the rain. The air was warm and humid, and what was a little water going to hurt? As I walked in the storm and became drenched with both the warmth of the air and the cleansing effect of the water, I felt my higher power, the God I truly believed in, wrap His love around me and drenched me in His Spirit and love. I had never felt His presence like that before.

I walked back to the rehab unit feeling as though He had everything under control. I had not been, and was not, alone through this. He was right there the entire time. I felt as though the rain had washed away some of the guilt, shame, regret and sins of defeat. That walk gave me the sense I had been given an opportunity to change my life, pick up my equipment and get back into the game of life refreshed and revitalized.

Later in the week I was released from the addiction inpatient clinic. With the help of others, I had now put two successful and large pieces of my recovery foundation into place. One piece was the Pain Rehabilitation Clinic and the other, the Drug and Alcohol Rehabilitation Clinic. For the first time in years, I began to feel the tide turning in my favor. Although I was not out of the woods, I knew I had gained a substantial amount of ground.

The next step in my recovery plan was for me to stay at a local hotel and attend the outpatient drug rehabilitation follow-up classes Mayo provided in the same building as the pain and drug rehab programs. Although I missed family and friends, and seemed so far from home, I knew I had to stay in order for me to have a greater chance at success.

Up to this point, I had been protected by staying in an inpatient clinic where I was somewhat protected from outside influences. Of course, not totally protected as evidenced by my poor decisions while a patient in the inpatient clinic. However, now I would be out on my own. I would have to deal with the realities of living back in the world and making wise and healthy decisions. This is where they say "the rubber hits the road."

By this time, I had built some trust with the staff at the drug rehab clinic, and was placing a large amount of trust into their hands and plan. I had done the hard work they asked of me and decided with all my heart to buy into the new way of life they were presenting.

A Changed Man

While attending the three week outpatient substance abuse program, I met several people like me, who had an addiction that had created havoc in their lives and caused their lives to become unmanageable. Some of my classmates had gone through the same inpatient clinic I had in Rochester, while others decided to try the outpatient clinic to see if it would be enough for them to find lasting success.

Everyone I met in the outpatient clinic was experiencing a different level of addiction. Some had been addicts for years, while others had just experienced their first negative life experience because of their addiction. I met a nurse who had been dealing with an addiction for several years. She had gone through the same experience I had, with attempts at rehabilitation centers. She also found herself using wherever she went and said she had even used while working at a hospital as a registered nurse.

Another individual was a legal aide, working in a law office. Although she was successful at her chosen profession, she found addiction weighing on her shoulders. As she shared her story, I could relate to many things I had in common with her. Due to a marriage break-up, she had wanted to numb her feelings and found by using alcohol and sleeping pills, she was able to do that.

I learned a great deal from these individuals who also became my friends. Although we had taken different routes in our lives and found ourselves with addiction issues for different reasons, we could relate, share our struggles and weaknesses, and know others in the group had gone through the similar experiences.

While attending the group sessions, our counselor, Karen, and other team members talked about different topics every day. The topics were meant for us to focus on, dive into as a group, and learn different ways of dealing with life on life's terms. Some of the topics were health, faith, emotional, relational, and physical aspects of recovery. Each day we would have a lesson of some sort dealing with one of these topics. What I found helpful was these lessons were not the normal boring teacher/counselor lectures, the leaders made sure every lesson required each of us addicts to be involved.

After almost three weeks of attending the outpatient clinic five days a week, I was scheduled to go home. Although I had done the hard work to get to this point, the thought scared me to death. I was still feeling the effects of withdrawal and had an uneasy stomach, bowel issues, dry mouth, vision issues, a mental cloud, and an immense fear of the future, relationships, work and life.

I had built some success in Rochester and had followed the instructions of medical professionals who invested their time and care into my well-being. I had bought into a recovery that was truthful, difficult, rewarding, realistic and most important, mine. However, I didn't know how I would handle home. Being sober was hard enough in the presence of the respected Mayo Clinic, but how would I do it at home without the daily groups, counselors, watchful eyes and others like myself? I would return home to begin a new life in the same environment I had left. The only thing changing was me. I was now a man clean of drugs and alcohol with the tools to learn to live with chronic pain and no excuses not to raise my game and become the man I was created to be.

Although I knew there would be struggles, I thought I would go home and surprise everyone with my new healthy lifestyle and wow them with my new found sobriety, integrity, honesty, openness and willingness to live a life free of drugs and alcohol. Little did I know some of those close to me back home would have to accept I was coming home a changed man.

Rehab Roller Coasters

By Sheryl Start

The first time Ken went into rehab I felt hopeful he would get the treatment he needed to reduce the pain meds and get back to real life. Little did I know what the results would produce. I took him to the doctor's office and it was decided to put him in a rehab. I knew it would not only be difficult for him, but also for me. I was left alone to take care of our three small children by myself. I also had to make sure I visited Ken while he was in the hospital. It was stressful trying to take care of the kids and make sure things were okay with Ken and his recovery.

I went to the hospital everyday feeling hopeful that progress was being made, yet I felt more and more disappointment with each visit. He never seemed to be out of the drug fog that put him there.

One day I was visiting Ken with his mom and dad. Ken thought it would be a good idea to start smoking instead of using drugs. I was appalled with the idea, but his dad thought it was a great idea since he was already a smoker. His dad jumped right up after Ken made the announcement and said let's go to the smoking room. I was in shock! I didn't marry a smoker.

His mom, dad and Ken jumped up and headed to the smoking room. I stayed. How could he think substituting one addiction for another was improvement? I refused to watch him smoke and I left the room. His mom came back out right away to sit with me, but I was completely disappointed. Later, I had a discussion with Ken and he assured me he would no longer visit the smoking room and would not pursue this new addiction.

Ken was in rehab for two weeks and during another visit we decided we would go to the hospital cafeteria. Ken was 6'5" tall and I was 5'5" tall. As we walked down the hall, he kept stumbling into the wall as I tried to keep him straight. What was happening? He was supposed to be getting better not worse. He could hardly stand up straight and his speech was still slurred. He was worse than when I first admitted him. I felt so discouraged. Here I was trying to be supportive, taking care of the kids and everything else that needed to be done by myself, and he was no better. How could I ever bring him home like this? I had no idea where to turn or what to do. I thought rehab would be the answer. His doctor in the rehab insisted he had to increase some of his meds due to the pain and suffering Ken was experiencing. Little did I know Ken had been manipulating his way to more and more pills.

Ken was released for two weeks and would then return to rehab for another two weeks with the same results. What was I going to do? This was just not working.

The first rehab had started in November of 1992 and went into December after the second two week stay. In January, we heard about a doctor in Grand Haven that was supposed to be really good. I made an appointment for Ken and arranged babysitting for the kids so I could take Ken to this new appointment. I watched him from the corner of my eye on the 20 minute ride to this appointment. He was lethar-

gic with his head down, not speaking and totally incoherent. In other words, he was stoned. We arrived at the office and took a seat. Dr. Mulder turned out to be a life saver. He told Ken what would happen if he was to keep him as a patient and how Ken would have to comply with him or he would not help. I was impressed right away, finally some help. I had prayed for some help with this situation and it had arrived in this doctor. I prayed Ken would agree with him and do as he asked. To my relief, Ken said he would do what Dr. Mulder asked.

Immediately he reduced the amount of pills Ken was taking. I wanted to cry with relief, here was someone who cared and wanted to help Ken come back from this addiction. I would have my husband back and my kids would have their dad back clean and sober.

I continued to drive him to and from Grand Haven. Gradually I began to see clear eyes and someone who was coherent enough to drive to Grand Haven by himself. Within six months Ken was doing well and back to his normal self, or so I thought. On one visit in June, Dr. Mulder announced he would be closing his practice in Grand Haven and moving out of state. Oh no, would things continue on this same path? We found another doctor again in Grand Haven, but things did not go well as time went on. Ken ended up back to his old ways as he found he could manipulate yet another doctor with his wit and charm. Here we go again.

I was becoming disillusioned with rehabs and what to expect. Why did Ken continue to keep going down that path? I knew nothing about addiction and was only trying to do what the doctors told me to do. I felt so frustrated and alone. Was his family not important anymore? Questions were all I had. Why? Why? Why? Why would he continue to do this? Didn't he know his wife and kids needed him? Did he not care enough about us to get help? I just did not understand. He had come so far with Dr. Mulder. What kept an addict an addict for so long? What was going on here? I had no one to tell me the answers. I knew no other addicts or co-dependents. I would learn what that term meant much later on as I never thought there was anything amiss with me. I did not even know this was considered a family disease. I would later learn a lot more about addiction and co-dependency.

With every rehab I had some hope at the beginning and then would end up feeling hopeless, discouraged and desperate trying to figure out what to do. While this was happening with Ken over the years, I still had all the responsibilities at home. I didn't have help from Ken, including finances. I struggled so much to make ends meet and never had a partner to discuss anything with in regards to money.

The kids got older and were involved with sports and Ken was a big part. He went to as many games as he could, but always with his pills. I was unaware of the amount he was taking. I knew he was using, but I was still a busy mother and also worked outside of the home. I was tired and just kept trying my best to protect my kids from seeing what was happening, and keep a somewhat normal life. My faith kept me in my marriage as I still loved Ken enough to think this marriage would survive and God would see us through. It would be a test for sure.

Ken's final rehab would be a real test for us both. He was at Mayo Clinic's Pain Rehabilitation Center for three weeks and would end up in their addiction clinic for the next two months. What ended up being a three week visit turned into three months. Our oldest son was married by then with a little boy, our middle son had graduated the previous year and was working, and our daughter was in high school. Time had marched on and we were still dealing with this addiction.

After talking to his counselor and deciding he would stay and get the help he needed, I finally felt hope again. This was the answer I had been waiting for. Ken had great respect for his doctor at Mayo, Dr. Hooten, and he developed great relationships with some of the patients and professionals in the addiction clinic. It was still tough at home but I felt we had found the right path.

My daughter and I went out to see Ken the last week of July. I was so excited to see him, but when we got there the doctors had already started to detox him and he was miserable. He was really sick and even though he tried to participate in things we wanted to do, he was miserable. I was feeling a bit discouraged. I felt he didn't want us there and was treating us as such. We were there for a week and I shed a few tears by myself. Would this never end? We left at the end of the week.

Before we left I had to check him in at the addiction clinic and as I left him at the door to the clinic I was hoping and praying this would be our answer. I felt so alone when I got back in the car. My daughter and I headed out of town and I tried to make the best of it, but I still felt so discouraged. Would this one be the one? Would I finally get my husband back?

Throughout his stay during the month of August the counselors would call to check on things at home to make sure I was doing okay. No one had done that in the past. Someone actually cared enough to check on me. I had not experienced that before and it was refreshing to feel somewhat important. They also shared Ken's progress and we had some conference calls, as well. I began to feel some hope again. Even though there were some struggles along the way it seemed things were coming along, even though it was slow. The counselors recommended that Ken continue on with after care for another month and Ken asked me to come out again. Did he miss me? I made arrangements to go back to Mayo Clinic in September, along with my mother. Her support had been critical for me for years. I knew others had been supportive as well, like my dad and stepmom, but they lived in Florida so their support was through constant prayer.

Mom and I made it to Rochester and checked in at the hotel with Ken. We both went to some support groups held at the addiction clinic and learned new things about addiction and the disease. We headed back home and I felt somewhat better after seeing Ken, clean and sober. I knew he had a lot of work to do, but I believed he could do it. I knew the end of his stay in Minnesota was getting closer and I was anxious to have him home.

He finally flew into Grand Rapid on October 4th, which was our 22nd wedding anniversary.

What I wasn't aware of was just what my role had become and how utterly unattractive my behavior had become. This was his problem. He had the addiction and I hadn't done anything wrong. Had I? It took me years to figure out who I had become and what was I going to do about it.

The Unfamiliar Familiar

I flew home October 4, 2007, the day of my twenty-second wedding anniversary. It was a warm, sunny Michigan day and I landed in Grand Rapids where my family met me at the airport. After greeting one another with smiles, hugs and kisses, we picked up my luggage, loaded up the car and headed toward my hometown of Muskegon.

It was fall in West Michigan and the colors were vibrant as we traveled down the highway. Along with my wife, my daughter-in-law Kristyn, daughter Sheri, and two-year-old grandson Jayden were in our Dodge minivan. I was so happy to see each of them and our conversation was light. We talked, laughed and it seemed like we took right off where we left off. There was just one huge difference, me.

As we drove, I chatted and laughed with the others, but I felt different. It felt as though I was in a cloud. My mind was unclear, I felt out of place and as if something was missing. My eyes even felt different. It seemed strange, but I had only been clean for less than sixty days and was still going through strong withdrawal symptoms.

After arriving at my house and unloading my luggage, the sense that I was only a visitor filled my mind and heart. The house seemed different, but I realized the house wasn't different, it was me.

I had not been clean and sober in that house in years. I had been gone for months and my home had become a hotel and rehab unit hundreds of miles away in a different state. My home had been with others who were like me. My family had become other addicts and pain patients, and I now found myself in this strange environment back home with those who loved me and missed me, but I felt like an outsider. It was not my family or those around me making me feel like I didn't fit in, it was me.

I didn't know how to act, feel, speak or behave around those I loved when I was not under the influence of something. Being sober around my family was a new, weird and uncomfortable experience. Tom and Karen, my counselors back at the Mayo Clinic, had made it clear this would happen to some degree, but I thought I would not have a problem returning home. This distorted thinking made me believe I would return and pick right back up with the great relationships I had left.

That night my kids, grandson, parents and some friends came over for pizza. As we sat at our dining room table we laughed, hugged, and caught up, I continued to feel like an outsider watching this happy and joyous event. I felt unplugged the entire time.

The next day, my wife had planned a drive to Manistee, a beautiful town about an hour north of Muskegon to celebrate our anniversary and allow me the opportunity to relax and enjoy sharing time together. It was a picture perfect West Michigan day with the sun shining, the fall foliage at its peak and the air a beautiful seventy degrees.

As we drove, I found it hard to think of things to say. Without the fog of drugs and their effects, I did not know what to do or say in these one-on-one situations with loved ones. It was an awkward ride for me, as I knew I had disappointed my wife in so many ways. Her trust for me had been shaken and I didn't know how long our relationship would withstand the pressures and trials I had brought upon it.

During our walk on the harbor, we talked about general things and enjoyed the beautiful day, vibrant colors along the water, boats sailing in the direction of Lake Michigan, and the ducks and geese paddling along the edge of the water. We walked through the town of Manistee and my wife, the never ending shopper, looked through the shops while I found a bench to sit on.

I felt like a fish out of water and didn't know where my journey would take me. It was like watching the world go on around me, but I was not part of it. I knew I had to once again become part of my environment, but was learning it would take time, effort and work.

My wife came out of an antique shop and we continued our walk down Main Street looking through different shops and stores. Later, we stopped at a restaurant and enjoyed a great dinner and began our journey home. While my wife drove, I shared how empty I felt and how I did not know where to go from here. I knew I had to do the work for pain rehabilitation and addiction recovery, but rebuilding relationships, my home life, church, work and everything else seemed so far away.

My wife stated she was proud I had taken the steps to attend pain rehab, inpatient and outpatient drug treatment, and made the decision to live a new life clean of drugs.

"You just have to take it one day at a time," she said. "Do what needs to be done and that's all." She made it clear no one had any expectations of me, other than to stay with the recovery course and if I did, the rest would fall into place.

"I just don't know where I stand with anything," I said. I was unsure of my career path, education, faith, where I stood with family and most important, I didn't know where I stood with our marriage. This conversation was a hard topic to approach.

"We'll pray," she said, "and in time there will be clarity." She stated it wasn't the time to think about our marriage, as I was just back home and had to adjust to everything.

Our conversation taught me I could be open with my wife without the world falling apart. I had always felt if I shared anything bad with those around me, things would fall apart or they would lose their temper, start yelling at me and walk out. I learned others could be stronger than I thought and handle much more than I gave them credit for.

The next morning, as instructed, I called my sponsor Dan and we made arrangements to meet at his office. I set a few attainable goals for the day, completed the daily stretching routine to maintain and increase the physical improvements I had learned, made a daily schedule to keep me focused and occupied, and also completed a daily reading and prayer.

I was alone at the house, had completed my morning exercise and routine, and was sitting in my recliner in the living room, feeling the same emotions I was feeling the day before. I felt a wave of oddness come over me knowing the drugs and alcohol I had collected, hoarded and highly valued were gone. I had nothing on hand to turn to in a pinch.

After a bit, I changed into shorts, a t-shirt and running shoes to complete the next task on my priority schedule, a five mile walk. I had started walking while in the Pain Rehab Center and felt it had assisted me in feeling better physically, and was a great stress reducer. I put my ear buds in, cranked up the music and began my walk, not in Minnesota, but right there in my own neighborhood.

Over the next few weeks, I had acclimated myself into a comfortable routine. However, the fog was still there and I still felt like a fish out of water. At times I would have liked nothing better than to run back to addiction. I was so thankful the Mayo Clinic had me set up with a sponsor at home while I was still there. He assisted me in transitioning from Minnesota to Michigan, and from addiction to recovery.

Dan and I had sat down together at his office when I arrived home and he asked me to call him every day just to check in. He also had me read the 12-step literature every morning and we began to meet to work on the twelve steps of the recovery program. Dan and I spoke about my cravings, emotions, doubts and fears, and how to combat them.

He was a perfect fit for me, due to his kindness, dedication to the program and humor. He could have me thinking seriously about my addiction issue one minute and have me laughing the next. He was easy to talk to, approachable and took recovery seriously. Dan was a perfect addition to my recovery puzzle, another piece that fit, and he assisted me in creating a picture that was becoming clearer.

I was now home, meeting with my sponsor, attending 12-step meetings on a daily basis, following through with the physical routine and daily schedule. Although my life was busy with recovery activities, I still had plenty of hard work to do and so many things to learn.

Just like I had had to learn to trust the others in my group, my family had to learn with me. After leaving treatment and returning home, I had committed my life to a 12 step program of recovery and change. The change included living a life of openness with my addiction, accountability and transparency. Living this new life would bring trust, but trust would not appear overnight. It had to be earned by not only saying what I would do, but doing it as well.

This process of building trust required me to return home from treatment and begin living a life that would piece-by-piece, brick-by-brick, rebuild the relationships between me and those around me. It required me to fill my schedule with meetings, counseling, regular exercise, family activities, household duties and work. In addition, I began the regiment of reading devotions, praying and meditating.

This new schedule was not easy to follow. Like before, I was often tempted to not attend or follow through; however, I had those around me cheering me on, supporting me, and expecting me to be where I said I would be. I was always tempted to skip meetings and appointments, but I did as I was told and little by little, this schedule began to pay off.

My family began to see I had learned a new way of living while in treatment. They also witnessed me doing the hard work of finding a sponsor, meeting with him on a regular basis, starting an exercise regimen, attending family and social functions, following through with more and more household duties and a big change in my behavior. I went from being a deceitful, selfish, temperamental and depressed individual, to an honest, open, active and dependable family member.

Step by Step
One Step at a Time

Since being home, I had taken care of my personal issues one item at a time. My next goal was to sit down and speak with my boss to see what the plan was for me to return to my job. My hope was to return to my work position now that I was actively in recovery and working toward a life of sober living. I called my boss and made an appointment to talk about my return to employment.

The next day, I found myself at the office where everyone gave me a warm greeting and I was happy to see everyone. After a few minutes of walking around the office and saying hello, I made my way to my boss's office for our scheduled appointment. I was nervous about returning, but it was the positive energy I felt that made me believe I would be returning to work in the next few days, or at the worst, in the next few weeks.

I spoke with my boss, Char, about my return home and trip to the Mayo Clinic, and then she talked about her plan for me to return to work. Char's plan and my plan were very different, but since she was the boss I knew I was going to have to change my plans to match hers. Char explained the importance of my returning to the job in a healthy and lasting fashion. She wanted what was best for both me and the organization and I needed to do whatever it took for me to succeed.

It was obvious Char had thought about my situation and concluded it was best for me to take a few months before returning to work. She said that since I was receiving Social Security Disability Benefits, she felt it would be smart for me to take my time in returning. She had made plans for me to volunteer at a local disability center to work with individuals who lived with and dealt with various disabilities.

As soon as I heard volunteer, I zoned out and assumed the worst. I did not see that Char was looking out for me and protecting me. I believed she was getting rid of me in the nicest possible manner. Char was a smart, wise and experienced professional who lived and worked by a no nonsense philosophy. She had worked with individuals with disabilities on a daily basis for years, was a licensed Vocational Rehabilitation Counselor and manager of the entire region. Even though I knew she had stuck with me, loved me and even protected me when I should have been fired, my sick mind thought she was just letting me down easy.

Although I smiled, shook my head and agreed with her throughout the entire meeting, I believed I was history and would end up on the outside of this office looking in. Char placed her plan into motion, and although I did not like it, I had to trust the process and do as I was told.

After leaving the appointment, I sat in my car for trying to process what Char had just told me. My heart and mind were going so fast, I had to allow myself a few minutes to calm down and let the information soak into my thick skull. My first thought was to use, knowing that would calm me down, but I realized that would mean destroying everything I had been working toward. I knew I was in a bad place, so I called Dan.

After speaking to him for several minutes, he had me calmed down and I began to see the purpose of volunteering.

Dan reassured me that Char had my best interest at heart and her plan made great sense. He added I had to trust others and their opinions at this point, as my thoughts and opinions were probably not trustworthy. He added it would be smart for me to run big decisions though him or other people I trusted.

I realized I had known enough to call Dan and share my struggle with him. That was progress for an addict like me. I had come to a point where I knew I had to reach out to others in order to get through a rough time, and make a decision based on common sense, and not my warped thinking.

That same afternoon, I received a call from Char. She told me she had been thinking more about my situation since I left, and along with making an appointment with Disability Connection, the center she thought would be a good place for me to volunteer, she also wanted me to make an appointment with a man who worked part-time in their office. He worked with groups that dealt with substance abuse and had his own professional counseling practice. She had a high level of respect and trust for this man and felt he would be able to help me build on my recovery and professional plans.

I wasted no time in making an appointment with this man whose name was also Dan Q. I had a brief conversation with Dan Q over the phone and made an appointment to meet with him in his office a few days later.

I continued to attend meetings daily and listened, shared and even took notes. I also continued reading recovery material, physical exercise and daily routines. Even though I was busy, I was still feeling like I was living in a cloud of mental fog.

I met with the director of Disability Connection and made plans to start volunteering for her organization. Together we decided I would volunteer three days a week and work with individuals who, like me, had various disabilities. I would be assisting individuals who needed assistance in filling out disability applications for Social Security Disability, filling out required forms for local government offices for varying assistance programs, helping people get in contact with other non-profit organizations which would assist them with living arrangements, food assistance, medical assistance, and several other special needs.

After meeting with the director, I felt a sense of success. Although my goal was to return home and go right back to my position with the State Rehabilitation Office, I could see how this volunteer position would allow me an opportunity to help others and regain strength, serenity, confidence and personal success in my own life. It was decided I would start the following Monday, bright and early.

The next day, I met with Dan Q. As I sat in the waiting room alone, my heart begin to beat faster and my mind ran faster and faster. This was a man trained and educated to work with individuals like me. To me, this was not just a regular meeting with a counselor, as this man worked with my employer. This appointment carried extra weight and I was nervous. How would I get through this appointment without being high and sedated?

While my mind was busy running through the possible things Dan Q could ask me, or the terrible things I had done in the past he might want to revisit, he came out and greeted me. He was a tall, quiet, middle aged man with gray hair. He smiled, shook my hand and led me back to his office.

Over time, Dan Q became a large part of my recovery as he allowed me the time, patience, grace, guidance, forgiveness, friendship, love and most important, the opportunity to get to know myself. He wasted no time getting me involved in the recovery process, which included getting to know myself, accepting who I was regardless of failures, addiction, physical ailments and limitations, character flaws, defects, self-doubt and loathing. Dan Q allowed me to take my time and gave me an arena where I could work through some difficult personal issues, which had stood in my path toward personal acceptance and success for years.

Dan Q operated his own practice, so I began working with him one-on-one once a week and it was a rough start on my part. When I first starting meeting with him, he asked the type of tough questions addicts hate to answer. Some of his questions were, "What ownership do you have in the problem?" "If you really want change, are you willing to make a plan and stick to it?" "Are you willing and ready to be completely honest with those you love?" "Are you ready to be completely transparent?"

After sharing with Dan Q each week about my struggles and challenges, he asked me, "What payoff are you receiving by continuing to think and behave in the manner you are?" Then, and still to this day, I struggled with trying to make everyone happy, doing what others wanted me to do, and acting in ways I thought others wanted me to act. In the meantime, I resented not being my true self. Dan would often ask me what payoff I was receiving for continuing in my thought and behavior pattern. Each time he asked me, it made me think more about what I wanted and if I was willing to change my thoughts and behaviors in order to get the change I wanted and needed.

As time progressed, Dan Q had me start attending a men's group. There were probably about six or seven men in this group who met every Monday night. They had one important thing in common with me: each had an addiction issue. While most of the men were alcoholics, there were a few addicted to prescription and other drugs. There were a few who were addicted to both drugs and alcohol.

Although I attended this group every week and listened to the other men share their personal struggles, successes and set-backs, it took me several months to feel comfortable and share in a deep and personal fashion. Dan facilitated the group and with his professional and no-nonsense attitude, made the weekly meetings one I began to value, look forward to, and even enjoy. For the first time in years, I was making friends with others much like myself. Not friendships with individuals who, in treatment, leave and return to their homes in other states, but lasting friendships where we could stay in touch with each other on a regular basis.

I also began spending time building my personal relationship with my higher power, the God of my understanding, the One who created me for a purpose, the One who showed me unconditional love, and the One who never would give up on me. I spent time reading, meditating, praying and in time, this relationship began to grow and produce the results He promised and I desired.

Things were going well and for the first time in my life, I had built a strong foundation for a lasting recovery. With help, I had begun building relationships with people and professionals who would assist me in becoming successful in my recovery. I was listening to others I trusted, meeting with them on a regular basis, and calling others when I needed to talk. I was speaking and sharing at meetings, and was clean and sober.

Stronger

Three months after arriving home and beginning to build a new life, I returned to Mayo Clinic for a follow-up workshop with the Pain Rehabilitation Center.

Returning to Rochester was like returning home as I had spent over three months in this city and made a number of new friends. The Pain Rehabilitation follow-up workshop was led by Michelle, one of the nurses from the program, and attending were individuals who had successfully completed and graduated from the program. Each of us were at different levels in our recoveries.

To begin with, we filled out questionnaires showing how we were handling various aspects of our lives while living in chronic pain. The questionnaires assisted the Pain Rehabilitation staff in knowing where we stood with our current levels of pain, anxiety and depression, compared to the levels the last time we saw them. We then took time to stretch each part of our bodies, just as we did each morning while attending the program. After stretching, Michelle took us to a meeting room where we introduced ourselves, telling the group where we were from and when we had graduated from the program.

There were eleven pain rehab alumni attending the follow up program and several of us had traveled a great distance, such as California, Arizona, Georgia and Canada, to attend the workshop. That was a strong testament to me of how important it was to stay plugged in to each other and to the professionals who could assist us in living healthy and successful lives.

During the workshop, Michelle asked us to share our recent successes with the group. It was inspiring to hear the successes of those who were walking again after being bedridden, being completely off narcotic and opiate medications, going to school or college, returning to work after long periods of not being able to work, attending family and social events, and just living in general.

Michelle then asked us about some of our concerns and struggles. As we went around the room, it was interesting to hear the different struggles and how I could relate. As a group, we were dealing with family issues, worthlessness, communication, mood issues, struggles with keeping up the physical exercise, returning to doctors for pain issues, lack of self-confidence, and going back on pain prescriptions.

As I listened, I became frustrated as it seemed some in the group just wanted to complain and return to their old way of thinking by catastrophizing their personal situations. It seemed they were looking for excuses to fail and reasons not to work toward a better way of life.

Despite my frustration, I learned I had come a long way and had to continue to move forward. I had to take what I needed and leave the rest. This group was another piece of my puzzle, a piece that was making my complete picture clearer and clearer.

After lunch, Michelle had us go around the room and share where we were with our exercise routines and if we had kept up the routine we had learned at the clinic. It was clear physical exercise was one of the harder things to keep up with when returning back home. Although several individuals were doing the stretches, most were not following through with the exercise routine we needed to do in order to deal with the chronic pain.

Since returning home, I had walked daily and found it to be a large part of my personal success in handling chronic pain and living with addiction. Walking gave me the time to slow down my emotions, be quiet and listen to music. I loved the time I took to walk, the natural high the exercise provided, and the calm mood walking put me in.

The last thing Michelle did with was lead us through a relaxation exercise. While attending the three week pain rehab, we ended each day with a relaxation exercise and that day in aftercare, Michelle selected an audio relaxation. The audio relaxation had us each relax in our chairs or sit or lay on the floor. The lights were turned down low and we began by picturing a beach. The facilitator then had us start on a grassy knoll where we could see the beach down an embankment and take off our shoes and walk down the wooden steps leading to the beach. Next, we were walking through the sand to the water and feeling the warm breeze and sun on our skin, and warm water on our feet and legs. This exercise lasted about 20 minutes and was used to help us find a few minutes of quiet, relaxation, and diversion from pain and stress in our lives. At the end, the facilitator brought us back to the present, had us open our eyes and sit still and quiet for a few extra moments, before Michelle turned the lights back on and we were brought back to the present moment.

Some had been sound asleep and surprised by the lights being turned back on. Others were content to stay in the same position with their eyes closed and their bodies in a relaxed state. I had always had trouble relaxing long enough to enjoy these relaxation techniques. While the facilitator was speaking and leading the group through the exercise, I was thinking about things not related to the exercise and found it almost impossible to bring myself to listen to the instructions or follow them for a few seconds. The best form of relaxation for me was walking, putting my ear buds in and turning on my music.

Michelle ended the day by asking if there were any after thoughts anyone had to share or if there was anything we missed. After a few moments of silence, Michelle excused us to go and said she hoped to see each of us soon at another aftercare session.

After returning to my hotel room, I thought about how grateful I was that I had crossed paths with the Pain Rehab Center. They had pointed my life in the right direction and I was actually clean, sober and following the instructions they had given me to live a successful and healthy life.

Next on the schedule for the day, was to attend an alumni meeting at the substance abuse treatment center, where I had graduated from three months earlier.

Coming Back

Since I had graduated from the substance abuse treatment center, there was a new batch of addicts in hopes of finding their own sobriety.

The way the alumni meeting worked was the treatment center would have the current patients come up with questions relating to substance abuse and recovery. Two patient, informative and respected former graduates facilitated the meeting and as the meeting started, the alumni and current patients sat in a large circle. The two veteran facilitators started by having each of us say our name and drug of choice. As we went around the circle and introduced ourselves, it was interesting to watch as the alumni said their name with confidence and a smile, while most of the new patients introduced themselves quietly, some slouching in their seats with no emotion.

After going around the room and introducing ourselves, one of the facilitators started with the first question written on the chalkboard. An alumni would volunteer to answer the question first and then we went around the room listening to each alumni answer the question.

One of the three questions was "How do you go home and build trust with family members and friends?" When this question got to me, I decided to pass, listen to the others and try to learn what I could to be more successful in this particular area.

I was only 90 days clean and with my history of abuse and relapse, I was in no position to give advice to others. Learning to know when to talk and when to remain quiet at meetings was a great step and new strength assisting me in becoming a better listener, since I was not always thinking so much about what I would say.

As an alumni that night, I learned by listening to the others who had traveled down this road of substance abuse and successfully maneuvered their way into real and true recoveries. I listened to others who had learned how to relate with others and built trust with family and friends by trial and error and time. As each of the other alumni spoke, I heard their real life experiences of how they learned from the 12 step program, their sponsors, literature, and their personal higher power, about how to become an individual centered on integrity, self-discipline and self-respect.

I also gained a great amount of insight from the patients as well. The questions they prepared for the evening were thought provoking. Having just completed the inpatient treatment center, I knew the questions were heartfelt and the concerns of real people much like me. No books, medical professionals or seminars could compare to both the questions and answers that come from addicts and addicts in recovery.

Since then, I have returned to the same alumni group on several occasions. Each time I return the facilitators are the same, the patients are different and many of the alumni are faces I recognize and have met before in this meeting or from another meeting in the past. No matter how I met them, we share a common bond in knowing that to not live in active recovery will lead to relapse, self-defeat and eventually death.

Now I share my life experiences of living in recovery, take each of the questions, thoroughly think them through, and share with the group how I have dealt with the problem or concern

I have also learned from the patients. You often hear in 12-step meetings, "The new person in the room is the most important." It is definitely true at the alumni meetings. Having the meeting right in the treatment center allows patients to ask and share what is on their minds and hearts. The questions, thoughts, concerns and their physical appearance, expressions and raw emotions bring me back to being in treatment. Hearing the patients share their doubts, fears and stories, takes me back to a point in life I never want to revisit and allows me to see that recovery is possible. I know this to be true because I can see it in the other alumni sitting around the room, and I can thankfully see it in myself.

That particular day, with its new information and the ability to plug back into an energy source that allowed me to recharge and reset my focus on recovery, with both pain and substance abuse, gave me a lift in self-confidence. I went to bed feeling good about life, about myself and where I was going.

Well, Hello Mr. Start!

After a restful night of sleep, I walked back over to the Pain Rehabilitation Clinic to meet with Dr. Hooten and was greeted by the smiling and familiar faces of the women who ran the front desk. I took a seat in the waiting room and watched the current patients go through their normal daily routine, the same routine I had followed when I was a patient. My thoughts started coming and going so fast, I had trouble keeping track of them and what they meant. *Had I done enough since leaving? Maybe I should be doing more.* My mind went from doubts to positive thoughts and right in the middle of my second thoughts, I heard Dr. Hooten's soft voice.

"Well, hello there Mr. Start," he said. I looked up and there he was in a navy blue suit, white shirt and tie. He greeted me with a warm smile and an extended hand. After a quick hello, he asked me to follow him down the hall to his office which was quiet, neat and orderly, much like him. I sat in a seat across from his desk and he took a seat in his black high backed chair. He was smiling and looking at me and my nerves calmed down. All the time I had spent worrying about this appointment and allowing my mind to spin, was a waste of time and energy.

Dr. Hooten began by asking about my family and then how I was doing. After catching him up, I told him I was doing much better than I expected

As I shared with him what I had been doing over the past three months, I heard myself detail the hard work I had done, my successes and accomplishments.

I have since returned to see Dr. Hooten every three to six months and share with him where I am with work, relationships, recovery, pain, faith, struggles and successes. He has assisted me in setting short and long term goals, looking at issues I am dealing with, and seeing different options.

Over the past seven years, Dr. Kaye, Dan Q, my sponsor Dan, and several family members and friends, have travelled with me to meet with Dr. Hooten and work on issues related to each of them and how that may affect or improve my success in recovery.

Dr. Kaye and Dan Q even spent two days on the Pain Rehab floor working beside the team to get a better understanding of the Mayo Clinic's philosophy on chronic pain, as well as the medical and psychological treatment of the patients.

My follow up appointments with Dr. Hooten have been a mainstay and a must in my recovery. He has listened to me through good and bad times, assisted me in living with chronic pain, and coached me forward into a life no longer controlled by chronic pain and substance abuse.

At one point, Dr. Hooten and some of his colleagues asked me to be involved in creating a DVD to educate others about the misuse and over distribution of prescription drugs. This DVD has been used in training medical professionals, and in substance abuse treatment centers. I have also traveled with Dr. Hooten to speak at medical training seminars including the Quality & Safety Forum, Prescriptions from a Patient's Perspective Conference at the Mayo Clinic in Rochester, MN; The Pain Medicine for the Non-Pain Specialist

Conference in Marco Island, FL; and Safe Opioid Prescribing, University of Michigan, Ann Arbor, MI.

Speaking has allowed me to share my experience of the dangers of prescription drugs. I needed to share not only the dangers of misusing the drugs, but also becoming an addict who was consumed with controlling his own medications and doing whatever it took to get what I needed. My main goal was to inform the general public and medical profession about the problem over-prescribing and misusing prescription medications has become.

Prescription medications took me down a path in life I never saw coming and right into the grips of a deadly addiction lifestyle.

Always Leave the Door Open

After returning from Mayo Clinic, my boss had me volunteering at a non-profit disability agency in town. After proving I could emotionally, physically and professionally handle the work and schedule while living in recovery, she allowed me to return to work, but not without sitting down with my manager Todd and Dan Q.

At this meeting, Todd stated that in order for me to return to work, I would have to agree to continue to see Dan Q one-on-one and live a clean and sober life. Todd made it clear that using drugs or alcohol would not be tolerated.

While Dan Q and Todd were talking to me, my mind was off and running with my addiction leading the way. As they stated that no drugs or alcohol would be tolerated and I would be responsible to meet separately with the two of them on a regular basis, I wondered why. Had they not seen the great work I had done since being home? Dan had met with me several times by then and my having to sign a contract was irritating. I did as they required and signed the contract stating I knew they would not tolerate any alcohol or drug use. I also agreed to continue to follow-up with Dan Q on a regular basis. The other stipulation was that I would meet with Todd once a month and let him know how I was doing.

By the time I left the meeting I was mad, sweating and felt as though they had no right to treat me the way they had. As an addict, I felt like everything was about me and they should have seen how great I was doing. In reality, they were looking out for me. My employer was making sure I was aware of the job expectations, personal goals, avenues of communication, and the clear costs for failing to remain clean and sober.

Meeting with Dan Q and following his instructions of meeting once a week in a group of men who were addicts, assisted me in growing as an individual and living a life in recovery.

Todd was a man of integrity and although I agreed to meet with him only because of the contract, I was blessed to have been given the time to utilize his strengths in my goal of recovery.

I was back working at the State Vocational Rehabilitation office as the Social Security Specialist. I helped disabled individuals understand the Ticket to Work program and other work incentives the government had in place to assist disabled individuals in returning to work. I was speaking to small groups in several offices when I was asked to speak at a job fair at the local community college for disabled individuals looking for employment. Speaking was one of my personal goals and I enjoyed speaking about things I was passionate about, like assisting others.

Todd was a Vocational Rehabilitation Counselor who had moved up to office manager. He and I met as agreed upon and I began to look forward to our meetings. Todd always had a warm smile and made me feel good about myself and my successes. After each appointment, I left feeling I was working in the right direction. Instead of talking about what I had done wrong and how I messed up my life with addiction, Todd always reminded me of my strengths.

On one occasion, he asked me if I had ever thought of becoming a Vocational Rehabilitation Counselor. I shared that working beside him and several other vocational rehabilitation counselors, I had started to think about returning to school and earning a Master's Degree in Vocational Rehabilitation Counseling. However, I had no idea what it would take.

Over the next few months as we met and chatted, Todd and I spoke more about the possibilities of my returning to school. He shared with me his experience at Michigan State University, where he had earned his degree for Vocational Rehabilitation Counseling. One day, he gave me the name of the Dean in that department and told me to call him to schedule an appointment. Todd had even called the Dean ahead of time and spoke with him about me.

After speaking with the Dean at Michigan State about my past, education, interests and goals, he and I agreed it was important to meet in person and he asked me to travel to Lansing. Was this for real? An addict like me having an interview with a Dean at Michigan State? Did I have a chance at a college like that? Could I pull work, recovery, school and family together and make it work without relapsing or doing something foolish?

I was truly seeing the positive results of living a clean life, even though I was still craving drugs and alcohol, as well as living with chronic pain. The cravings would come and go and sometimes they were so strong, my body would go into cold sweats and I had to do something to distract myself. Then I would call my sponsor or a friend, go exercise, or drive to a local McDonalds, sit in the lobby and drink a few Diet Cokes©. For the pain, I used the tools I was taught at the Pain Rehabilitation Clinic by staying focused on goals, exercise, stretching, deep breathing, and being willing to adjust my schedule to meet my reality. Using these skills assisted me in getting through some tough times. I also found acupuncture was a great help for the back pain and anxiety.

Too Many Choices

Sitting in the Dean's office at Michigan State University was a day that made me feel like hard work pays off. After speaking with the Dean about my skills, experience, education and life in general I was aware of just how much I had accomplished in a short time. Although I was excited about the opportunities Michigan State and their program may provide, the interview provided me with a clear and realistic view of myself.

I could succeed without drugs and alcohol, and chronic pain was not who I was. I was a smart, talented, outgoing, fun and caring man who had a lot to offer society. I was a man who cared deeply about others and wanted to help those who were much like me, people looking for a path that led to success regardless of life experiences and various disabilities.

After the interview was completed, I left Michigan State with new options and new opportunities. I had learned a great deal about the Masters Program for Vocational Rehabilitation Counselors and believed I matched what they were looking for in a student. I left, believing the Dean felt I was a good fit because he told me about a competitive scholarship program they offered, and then gave me the application and instructions on how to apply for it. In addition, he congratulated me on my past educational accomplishments, recovery success and living with chronic pain. He made it clear my personal experience would assist me in the field of vocational rehabilitation counseling.

I went back to work and spoke with Todd about my interview and he encouraged me to apply for the scholarship and added he would do anything he could to help. The scholarship instructions required me to have three reference letters so I asked Todd, Char and my addiction counselor Dan to write them for me. I also gathered my educational transcripts, wrote a letter stating why I would be a good candidate for their program with a full ride scholarship, and sent it on its way well before the deadline. I was hoping for the best, but not expecting miracles, and dumbfounded I was even being considered.

Meanwhile, I continued to work and stayed busy with work, family and recovery. Living life on life's terms was not easy, but I was beginning to find success one piece at a time and learn how to live life without the use of drugs and alcohol. As I waited for a decision on the educational opportunity, I continued to move forward.

Who would have thought my accident, so long ago, would have had such an effect on my life. Not only did the accident cause me to go through several physical challenges, surgeries, life threatening infections, internal pumps, stimulators, multiple hospital stays, addiction issues, several rehab stints and mental issues, such as depression and anxiety, but it also opened a career path for me I never saw coming. As the saying goes, "Sometimes the biggest blessings are disguised." How true that was.

At the time of the accident I was working at a local factory as a visual inspector of automobile parts and attending college part-time to become an elementary school teacher. I was the father of two beautiful little boys, not knowing I would soon be blessed with a beautiful little girl as well. That cold, icy and dark February morning back in the winter of 1991 would forever change my life direction in every possible way.

About three weeks after sending in the application, letter of intent and transcripts to Michigan State University, I received a letter of acceptance to the college, and a notice that I had been selected as one of the few scholarship recipients for the Vocational Rehabilitation Counseling program. After realizing I had been selected, my heart skipped a few beats. Was this for real? I was now a Michigan State Spartan! The man who had been through eight drug rehab units was now going to attend Michigan State University on a full ride scholarship.

I had gone from a visual inspector in an automobile plant, to a disabled drug and alcohol addict, to a man who was now about to begin a new career as a Vocational Rehabilitation Counselor!

I thought I had it figured out and had a clear, smart and realistic plan. I would continue to work for the State of Michigan in the capacity of a Social Security Specialist, attend Michigan State University three times a week, graduate in two years, and hopefully land a Vocational Rehabilitation Counselor position with my current employer.

I started attending classes at Michigan State and was thrilled to be back in college knowing I had a clear and precise plan. I believed I had found my way, and I would graduate and have a happy and lasting career.

Once again, everything changed with one single phone call. One day at work, I received a phone call from the local Social Security's area manager who had attended one of the presentations I had done for my current job. My topic was the Social Security Administration's Ticket to Work Program. I was unaware she was in the audience. She told me she had been impressed with my presentation a few years earlier, and had kept me in mind for a position at Social Security. The government had now approved the hiring of a few additional employees and she asked if I would be interested in applying. I was speechless. I had wanted a job so I could be successful and everything was happening so fast.

I wasn't sure how to respond to her. I wanted to work for Social Security, but I had already decided to attend college and work toward a career in Vocational Rehabilitation Counseling, a career I was excited about.

I spoke with my boss Char, my manager Todd, and my drug addiction counselor and sponsor, and decided I had nothing to lose by applying. I sent in my resume, with no expectations. I continued to attend classes, work full time and move toward my goal one step at a time.

The following week I received a call from the Area Assistant Manager for Social Security. They had received my resume and were requesting that I come in for an interview for a position. I wanted to turn the interview down. I was happy with my current position with the State of Michigan, my college classes and my clear goal of becoming a Vocational Rehabilitation Counselor. However, I asked if I could get back with her later in the day to decide on a good time for an interview. She agreed.

Now what? I had set my plans, made a big decision and now this opportunity had presented itself. I decided I would return the call and turn down the interview. Just then Char walked by.

"Guess who just called me?" I said. I told her Social Security had just contacted me and wanted to set up an appointment for a job interview. Char's eyes lit up.

"When is the interview?" she asked.

"I told her I would call later with a good time, but I'm going to turn down the interview."

Char's eyes went from delight to frustration in seconds.

"Follow me," she said. We went to her office and she shut the door.

I had seen Char like this several times before with me, but not since I had been clean. She sat behind her desk and leaned over.

"What are you thinking?" she asked. Char told me I should never pass up an opportunity to interview for such a job. She also stated that I didn't know what kind of opportunity an interview would bring with it.

"Get back to your desk, call them back and set up the appointment to interview for that open position," she said.

As always, when Char told me to do something, I did it. I called Social Security back and made the appointment for the interview. Two days later I was sitting in an office with three management level employees at Social Security interviewing for a Social Security Claims Representative position.

After listening to the job requirements and responsibilities, the position seemed to match my talent and skill set. As a Claims Representative, I would assist the public with general Social Security questions and applying for one or more of the entitlement programs offered by Social Security.

I would have the opportunity to assist people who had various disabilities and were applying for Social Security Disability. As I learned more about the position my interest was piqued, since this sounded like something I could see myself doing and would be good at.

After an hour long interview, I left feeling confused. Why did Char encourage me to attend this interview? Now I was torn with indecision. Char had told me that I should never turn down an interview, or an opportunity to learn about other opportunities. However, as I left the interview I felt the "what ifs" enter my thought process. What if I did get a second interview or, heaven forbid, what if I was offered the position? What about the decisions I had made up to that point? I felt I was on the right path to success, working for the State of Michigan and attending Michigan State University to earn my Master's Degree in a field I felt matched my talents, background, and abilities. Now I had another huge decision to make.

Although I was going through a state of the "what ifs" after the interview, I also felt a great sense of accomplishment. I had just interviewed for a position with the Federal Government and felt the interview went great. With a sense of pride, I was able to speak of my educational, professional and personal accomplishments. I was able to answer the questions asked of me truthfully and with pride. I did not have to lie, mislead or manipulate and felt like as though I had just made friends with three new people. Life without recovery would have never allowed me to experience this sense of success and accomplishment.

I ran back to my boss, Char, and filled her in on my interview. She was all smiles and never questioned or doubted I would have anything but a great interview. Char believed in me and has been one of the people in my life who helped me begin to believe in myself. She and I talked about my interview and the opportunity it might provide. I shared with Char my feelings about the "what ifs" and she reminded me to take one day at a time. We talked about the job being in my hometown, the financial difference between working for the Social Security Administration and the beginning pay of a Vocational Rehabilitation Counselor.

She knew I was struggling with the idea of changing my plans and she assured me that Michigan State would be there later, if I decided to stop for this job.

"Take it one step at a time," she said, "and just continue to work toward a life of success." She laughed and added, "Just don't screw it up."

Two days after my interview, I received a call, not for a second interview, but to offer me the position. I was thrilled and confused at the same time.

This was a big decision for me. I wanted to continue with my plan of receiving my Master's Degree and finding stability. At the same time, this job offer seemed too good to pass up, with its stability, income, insurance, and the ability to assist others with disabilities.

After speaking with Char, Dan Q (my addiction counselor), Dan (my sponsor), my wife and parents, and with plenty of prayer, I decided to take the job.

I have since gone through the training, mentoring and probation period, and have been working for the Social Security Administration for nearly five years. Working for Social Security has been both an honor and joy. I have had the opportunity to serve countless others and hopefully shine some light on other lives, like those in my past have done for me. In addition, some of the people there who have added to my success have been amazing.

I shared my struggles with addiction and pain with my boss, David, and he has done everything in his power to assist me in reaching personal and professional goals. Although I have gotten under his skin a time or two with self-doubt, he has always been there to reassure me I had everything it took to be a great claims representative.

Another significant person in my work life has been my mentor, Vicki. She believed in me from the start and to this day is a huge part of my daily success. She is not only my mentor at work, but I consider her to be a great friend who is truly there when I need her, in good times and bad.

Five years has passed since I made the decision to take this job. Now, as I look back, I realize it was the right decision. Social Security, my managers, co-workers and the public I work with, have added to my confidence, sense of self-worth, purpose in life, ability to live with addiction and chronic pain, and have been there to cheer me on the entire way.

A Sad Reminder

As a claims representative for Social Security, it was my responsibility to take new disability claims from individuals who wanted to apply. In advance of the appointment, they were asked them to bring in a list of their physical and mental disabilities, as well as a complete list of the doctors, specialists, counselors, hospitals, clinics or other physical and mental professionals they had worked with in the past, or ones they had appointments with in the near future. In addition, we asked each claimant to bring a list of medications they were taking. Disability claims were much easier to complete, process and expedite, if the claimant came to their scheduled appointment with this requested information.

One of these cases made me think about my past, present, and my future recovery. I called an individual over the intercom system at work, asking her to come to my desk from the reception area. As I waited, I could hear her speaking as she walked down the long hallway of other interviewing desks and closer to mine. As soon as I made eye contact with the claimant, I knew I was dealing with a person either over medicated or addicted to medications or drugs. She was a young woman, maybe in her late 20's, and she was with a male friend who had driven her to this appointment. The claimant's eyes were blood shot and half shut, her body was limp, her mouth hung slightly open, she appeared to be in another world mentally, and she spoke with a soft voice. I knew of this world and in an instant it brought me back to where I once lived.

I introduced myself and then read her the legal attestation about giving us truthful answers and how she would be legally responsible for giving us false information; a routine I had to follow for each claimant. As I looked to the claimant for her response to the questions, she had her eyes closed and her mouth was slightly open. Her friend asked her if she agreed.

"Yeah," she said as she opened her eyes.

As I was preparing to enter the required personal information into the computer, she tossed a white shopping bag tied in a knot to keep the contents from falling out, onto my desk. I continued entering information and asking her general questions. Getting answers was difficult due to the claimant not being completely alert.

Somehow, we managed to get through the initial application for disability and moved to the medical portion where we took the medical information the claimant provided. Then we filled out the necessary information for the determination committee to make a decision based on correct and current information. By this time, I was feeling frustrated with the claimant. I had learned she had a bad back, issues with depression and anxiety, and was taking a lot of medications.

As we worked our way through the medical information, she was continually in and out of consciousness and I saw more of my former self in her every minute. This had caused old feelings I hated, yet missed, to rise up. As much as I have fought addiction over the past five years, I still had a part of me that was jealous of this sick, sad, disoriented and drugged woman. Why? Maybe it was the feeling of having no responsibility or maybe it was the high. Maybe it was not having to deal with reality. I didn't know, but it was creeping up in me. We continued with the interview.

Q: What is your disability?

A: I have pain in my back and feel sad most of the time.

Q: Could you elaborate on that?

A: I really can't tell you why I hurt or feel bad or sad.

Q: Were you ever injured causing your back to hurt or is there anything else in your history which possibly caused the back pain.

A: No.

Next, I asked about the depression. She stated she felt sad, told her physician and he placed her on meds for the condition and for her back pain. According to the claimant, she had no medical testing for her back issues and her doctor placed her on pain meds hoping it would cure her problems.

The next section on the application was about the medications she was taking. She pushed the white plastic bag in my direction and told me it contained her medications. When I untied the knot in the bag, I was astonished to find countless prescription bottles, all for depression and back pain.

As I reached into the bag and began to take the orange bottles out and set them on my desk, I felt my heart race and mouth water. After they were lined up on my desk, I began listing them one by one into the computer. As I picked up each bottle up, I read name of the drug, the date prescribed, dosage and prescribing physician. It made me feel like a kid in a candy store. However, I pulled myself back to reality and with a racing heart, sweaty palms and shaky legs, I listed each medication. They included OxyContin, Vicodin, Xanax, Klonopin and others I had misused on a regular basis. I even found myself looking at the warning labels on the bottles and getting a quick rush, knowing from past experience that some of these were my favorites, due to these listed dangers. After listing twelve different medications from the same physician, I loaded them back into the plastic bag, tied it up and shoved it back across the desk. It was then the claimant's friend stated, "No wonder you're always zoned out." He was right.

I completed the application process, finalized the information and sent them both on their way. However, the story did not stop there for me.

After she left our office, I was still feeling the effects of just holding the bottles that had contained the pills that almost took my life, pills I would have given my life for only a few years before. My mind was a blur and my heart continued to race until I got up, walked over to a co-worker and began to talk about another subject.

It was amazing how the small pills had made such an impact on me that day. Why? Was it because I loved the feeling they gave me? Did I miss them because they were my only friends and relieved my pain? Maybe it was the way they had allowed me to sleep all the time and escape reality. Or, was it the amazing guy I thought they made me? I didn't know, but they made a lasting impression on me, an impression I had been battling for almost five years; a battle I was not willing to lose.

Addiction is a serious illness that never goes away and I knew I needed help fighting this illness. I had to continually be on guard, knowing my addiction was always there, strong and willing to reappear at any time. All I had to do was give it an opening. In the past, I was willing to give up my short-lived sobriety for the high a handful of pills would give. However, over the past five years, I had grown as a person and realized I could not give in and go that route again. Whenever I thought about taking the next handful of pills or the next shot of alcohol, I played the tape forward and thought about the serious consequences one use would bring. It didn't take me long to play back the memories and see the sadness, heartache, defeat, failure and frustration each use brought. Even though I could still idolize the high, I now hated and detested the low that both drugs and alcohol brought to my life.

Time to Trust the Process

Although I was not responsible for the auto accident I was involved in over twenty years ago, I was responsible for the misuse, manipulation and lack of responsibility that caused my addiction to prescription drugs. In addition, I take full responsibility for my poor choices to buy, sell and trade prescription drugs on the street and my addiction to alcohol. It was my choice to begin shooting the cinnamon schnapps into my veins; no one was standing there forcing me to do these stupid activities.

However, my goal with this book is to shine some light on the problem of misuse, over-prescription, and lack of care with prescribing medications. There are doctors who are dedicated to their patients, profession and personal integrity. However, there are also doctors who don't take the time to get to know their patients, their needs, concerns and comprehensive health issues.

So many healthcare institutions are now requiring doctors to see a certain amount of patients in a particular amount of time. Although these requirements may help the time spent in the waiting room, I don't believe these requirements allow the doctor to get to know his or her patients on a deep level. What is more important, quantity or quality?

I left certain rehabilitation units with more medications than when I arrived. I spoke with doctors who did not even read my chart before entering the examination room. I met doctors who wrote prescriptions for lethal medications without knowing my past history and once, I was even scheduled for the wrong surgery.

Between the physicians not taking the time to know their patients, and the patients manipulating and misusing like I did, we have a huge problem in our country.

Addiction is a sad, lonely and miserable existence. Drugs and alcohol lure you in with the promise of a better tomorrow and once you are hooked, the addict begins to dread each and every new day.

I am one of the few people who has been able to remain clean and sober for a length of time and it is due to the twelve-step programs I have attended, the doctors and medical professionals who have followed up with me on a regular basis, a loving and patient family, prayers, a God who loves me and my honesty, open-mindedness and willingness to let go and let God.

Since leaving my last rehab visit at the Mayo Clinic, I have had countless blessings in my recovery. However, I have also have had to deal with situations that could have thrown me off my path to recovery.

One of those was losing my father in the spring of 2011. Life doesn't seem the same without his big and powerful personality. I also lost my father-in-law, Jerry Oosterhart, who was a big supporter and never gave up on me. Just knowing he was there made a huge difference. My mother, Joyce Start, was diagnosed with breast cancer and has undergone chemotherapy and radiation. Never in my life did I think I could handle seeing my mom, one of the closest people to me, undergo such a health crisis.

Although recovery has caused me to live in reality and go through such struggles, living a sober life has allowed me to be present for each of these hardships. I was there when my dad fell ill and when he asked me, the night before he died, if I realized how beautiful my mother was. I was also there when he told my mom he loved her for the last time. I spoke at my father's funeral and my words were heartfelt, true and sincere, as I was sober, clean and healthy.

I was also lying in bed the night we received the call my father-in-law had passed away in Florida, so I was able to support my wife during her loss.

I was at the hospital when my mother had her cancerous tumor removed. I was at the appointment when they told us she needed chemo and I was there when she walked in with her blond wig for the first time. I was there, no drugs, no alcohol, and no bullshit. I had to live life and accept things for what they were, just like everyone else.

Since living in recovery, I have also undergone jaw surgery to correct an issue from a previous auto accident, a deviated septum and sinus surgery. Previously, these surgeries would have had me excited about the drugs during and after the surgery. However, I was honest with the doctors, which meant I did not need prescription medications, and none were prescribed. I can't say drugs were not on my mind, but I can say they were not in my system. It was a huge deal for me to get through those surgeries without medications.

Since being home, I was involved in yet another serious auto accident. On May 31, 2012, I was coming home from a 12-step meeting and waiting at a red light when I was rear-ended by a drunk driver. The impact totaled my car, and caused me to hit my head and face on the sun roof. The drunk driver fled the scene, but was eventually caught and charged. I was rushed to the hospital where the emergency room doctor sewed up a deep gash over my left eye and nose.

Little did I know, I had received a concussion that would lead me down a lengthy recovery at Mary Free Bed

Rehabilitation Center in Grand Rapids, Michigan. While under their care, they worked with me one-on-one for cognitive, physical and vocational rehabilitation. I was also scheduled with a psychologist who has since become inspirational in my life, assisting me in staying on track and living with the chronic headaches the head injury caused.

This accident and head injury threw me off my game. I was working full time, living successfully in recovery with chronic back pain. Life threw me another curve ball and I had no choice but to accept it and make the best of it.

The ironic thing was that I was hit by a drunk driver on the way home from a 12-step meeting, where I had just shared about having cravings that day. The difference between me and the driver, who hit me, was I had given in and accepted that my life was out of control and I needed to trust and believe there was a God of understanding who would restore my sanity. Although I still was experiencing cravings, I had the tools to know the difference between a craving and a true need.

My prayer is that, through this accident, which we learned was not the driver's first alcohol related accident; he too has learned and accepted he has a problem that could cost him his life and others' lives as well. Although I missed almost a year of work due to my injury, I have forgiven this man and moved on from that rainy May evening.

Seven years after leaving the Mayo Clinic's Rehabilitation Center, I am still plugging away at making physical exercise a high priority. I joined the YMCA in town and came to enjoy my daily walks on the track, swimming in the pool, sitting in the steam room and feeling the natural high exercise brings. Thankfully, Dr. Kaye felt I could benefit from having a physical exam and evaluation at the Shoreline Sport and Spine Center (now i'move) in Spring Lake, Michigan to see if they could help me work toward my goals of physical fitness.

After undergoing an evaluation and assessment from the Director of Athletic Training at i'move, Mike Braid, it was no shock to learn my body was not moving like it should. Since having the spinal fusion and tons of other back surgeries, my back, hips and legs were in desperate need of stretching and exercising. Mike made a plan with me for a physical routine. He believed he could assist me in getting a bit more flexibility and moving more may help some of my chronic pain. Under the watchful eye of Mike and i'move, I am now running five miles, three times a week on a machine called an Alter G. I have never been a great athlete nor have I been a runner, but with the aid of this weight calibrated treadmill, I have worked from walking to running. I have increased to running three times a week, five miles a run, at 80 percent of my weight. This treadmill has allowed me to reach goals of running I never thought possible.

Another experience that has aided me greatly in being successful was attending a week long treatment at Onsite Workshops in Cumberland Furnace, Tennessee. While at Onsite, I was afforded the opportunity to work through some of the effects of the trauma I had experienced through my multiple auto accidents. I was also given the opportunity to work through personal issues, such as addiction, personal relationships and childhood incidents that had affected and changed my life.

I am grateful for my time at Onsite and have to say thank you to Myles Addox, the President and CEO, along with my counselor, Linda, for teaching me I am worthy and valued. She taught me to trust the process of recovery and to continue to move forward and love myself. My experience at

Onsite has made me evaluate my life, relationships and make changes I feel are needed to be truly successful.

Accepting My Worth

For years, I lived life believing I was not as good as everyone around me, or as smart, talented or worthwhile. I have always been a follower, one who has had trouble speaking my mind, sharing what I believe or standing up for what I believe to be right. Instead, I usually rode on the coat tails of those around me, assimilating their thoughts and beliefs as my own. I learned at a young age that to speak your mind or to go against the grain was a tough thing to do and something not always tolerated.

After living with pain and addiction issues, I moved through stages of recovery that have assisted me in improving my self-image and allowed me to become an individual with his own identity, belief system and voice. Recovery and those I chose to associate with have taught me I am a worthwhile individual worth fighting for. Recovery has taught me life is not centered around me. I was not placed here on earth only for my sake, but to help those around me become the best they can be as well. By becoming aware of this fact, I have begun to reach out to others in a sincere manner. In turn, this has brought me an increased amount of self-worth. I do have a purpose and I am here for a reason.

I have also learned through recovery I am not the one in control, my higher power is in control. Before my accident and addiction issues, I always viewed my higher power as a loving God, but also a judgmental God who watched and judged every move I made.

My personal faith in Jesus, as my Lord and Savior, has been a constant in my life and I have no doubt, He alone, carried me through the past 50 years. I accepted Jesus as my personal Savior when I was a young child and since then, have trusted Him to lead my life. I have not been the faithful follower and have deviated from His path several times, but I know without a doubt, I have never deviated from His love and acceptance.

However, through my personal recovery, I have learned God created me to love and praise Him, not to watch me squirm with each wrong choice I made. He has gifted me with an insurmountable level of grace, which allows me to stand and say He loves me and I am forgiven and precious in His eyes. However, God has taught me how important accountability and personal responsibility are for me to live a happy, healthy and honest life. Learning I am loved by God and precious to Him, has allowed me to accept myself for how He created me, flaws and all.

God's grace picked me up and carried me countless times throughout the years. His love, acceptance, patience and promise of a better tomorrow, has given me hope in dealing with physical pain and addiction and living with each day's struggles. I have been judged harshly by myself and others, but I know who created me and I know He created me to love Him and praise Him, not only during the good times in life, but also during the storms of life. He created me to love others and respect, honor and assist them in any way I can.

My story will go on. I will continue to live in recovery one day at a time. I will meet up with new challenges and use the tools I have gained to deal with them in a successful manner. I will laugh, love, cry, live and appreciate each moment. I will move forward and build on my mental, personal, professional and physical successes, to strive toward a life that is an instrument that can be used by others in hope of finding a better tomorrow.

I still have a long way to go, but I can now begin to accept who I am today and love myself. I will continue to become who God created me to be—the Ken who loves, laughs easy, enjoys others, works hard, lives for the moment, loves God and not only loves himself, but desires to become the best Ken I can be.

...Now

The well-dressed man in the audience stares at me.

"I'm not trying to be cocky," I say. "In fact, I'm terrified just being in this room with so many brilliant people." I swallow hard. "But if my story will help just one doctor think twice about over-prescribing opiates, it may keep someone from becoming an addict...like me."

The man sits back down and we continue with more questions that spark debate and conversation. After several minutes, we end our segment of the presentation.

Dr. Hooten gives the floor back to the host of the conference and we both return to our seats in the front row of the auditorium. I wipe the sweat off my forehead and try to control my shaking hands. Dr. Hooten pats my shoulder and gives me a smile that tells me we did well.

Later, as I walk out of the auditorium, several medical professionals approach and thank me for being so open and honest about my addiction and self-defeating behaviors. Knowing Dr. Hooten and I have shared the truth about what a large number of patients are doing to manipulate medical professionals, makes this experience worthwhile.

Too many prescriptions are being written, too many are for people taking pills for the wrong reasons, too many patients are seeking and searching in doctors' offices, med stops and emergency rooms for drugs that will feed their nonstop addiction for their next high. Sadly, there are families losing loved ones to overdoses on prescription medications.

My hope is that my story shines a light on a problem that has become an epidemic in our country.

About the Author

Ken Start was born and raised in Muskegon, Michigan. He graduated summa cum laude from Cornerstone University in Grand Rapids, Michigan with a BS in Business Management and Ministry Organizational Leadership.

He studied Vocational Rehabilitation Counseling at Michigan State University in Lansing, MI.

Ken works for the Social Security Administration as a claims representative working with, and assisting, individuals living with various physical and mental disabilities and limitations.

Married to wife Sheryl for 29 years, he has three children, two special daughters-in-law and four grandsons.

Ken has shared his personal experience with drug and alcohol addiction to educate crowds and individuals about the dangers and long-lasting ramifications of addiction on the body, life and families this widespread disease preys upon. He has spoken at the Quality & Safety Forum, Prescriptions from a Patient's Perspective Conference at the Mayo Clinic in Rochester, MN; The Pain Medicine for the Non-Pain Specialist

Conference, Marco Island, FL; and Safe Opioid Prescribing, University of Michigan, Ann Arbor, MI.

He has also been a regular speaker at faith-based adult and teen conferences.

If you are interested in having Ken speak to your group, please contact him at kenstart07@gmail.com.

A Prescription for Addiction

can be purchased online at amazon.com
or directly from the author at
kenstart07@gmail.com.

Discounts available for multiple book orders.

A Prescription for Addiction

is also available as an eBook
on Kindle and the Nook.

Speaking Engagements

Author Ken Start is available and willing
to share his story with your group.

Please feel free to contact him at
kenstart07@gmail.com for scheduling information.